Even MORE *Than* MONEY

Five Ways to Design Your Financial Life

EDITED BY **Shanna Due**

CURATED BY

Taylor Schulte & **Justin Castelli**

Harriman House

HARRIMAN HOUSE
3 Viceroy Court
Bedford Road
Petersfield
Hampshire
GU32 3LJ
GREAT BRITAIN
Tel: +44 (0)1730 233870

Email: enquiries@harriman-house.com
Website: harriman.house

First published in 2026 by Harriman House, an imprint of Pan Macmillan
EU Representative: Macmillan Publishers Ireland Ltd, 1st Floor, The Liffey Trust Centre, 117-126
Sheriff Street Upper, Dublin 1, D01 YC43
Associated companies throughout the world
www.panmacmillan.com

Paperback ISBN: 978-1-80409-124-1
eBook ISBN: 978-1-80409-125-8
Audio ISBN: 978-1-80409-450-1

British Library Cataloguing in Publication Data
A CIP catalogue record for this book can be obtained from the British Library.

01

Printed and bound by CPI Group (UK) Ltd.

Cover design by Charlotte Smith. Adobe stock images used.

Praise for
Even More Than Money

"If you've ever wondered what financial planning looks like when it's really working, start here. Inside are twenty real stories from advisors who stopped pretending they had all the answers and started telling the truth about what happens when money meets life."

—**Carl Richards, author, *Your Money***

"*Even More Than Money* is a powerful reminder that true wealth isn't measured by what you accumulate, but by how intentionally you use your resources to live with purpose."

—**Jamie Hopkins, CEO, Bryn Mawr Trust Advisors**

"By sharing real stories and real lives, *Even More Than Money* brings humanity to financial planning in a way that is both powerful and deeply needed. It will resonate not only with financial professionals, but with anyone who understands that money is never just money."

—**Cary Carbonaro, CFP®, MBA, author, *Women and Wealth***

"*Even More Than Money* offers twenty stories told firsthand by the advisors who were in the room; what they quietly reveal is that every money decision is really a life decision (and vice versa). Approachable at first, and genuinely transformative."

—**Tim Maurer, CFP®, RLP®, author, *Simple Money***

"The love these financial planners have—for their calling, for their clients—illuminates their deeply felt stories. Readers will come to this book for the education, but they'll stay for that love."

—**Nick Murray, author, *Simple Wealth, Inevitable Wealth***

"Money can make your life better, easier, and more comfortable in times of crisis; the key is to have a real plan and an advisor who is comfortable pushing you to do what is best, even when you cannot see it at the time."

—**Matthew Halloran, TEDx speaker and author, *Shut the F Up and Listen***

CONTENTS

INTRODUCTION

WHAT IS MONEY REALLY FOR?

IT'S A QUESTION that deserves more than a textbook answer. One of Taylor's clients discovered this the hard way. She had $5 million in the bank. She couldn't sleep at night. "What if I run out?" she asked, staring at her seven-figure portfolio statement.

Her anxiety wasn't unusual. Of the 110 high-net-worth families Taylor serves, nearly all of them have more money than they could ever spend. These are people with $2 million, $5 million, even $10 million saved. Yet 90% still wake up anxious about running out of money.

Welcome to *Even More Than Money: Five Ways to Design Your Financial Life.* This is Justin Castelli and Taylor Schulte, inviting you to explore 20 real-life stories gathered from financial advisors' most profound client experiences.

Why do so many successful people feel this disconnect? As Taylor often observes, the type of person it takes to save that kind of wealth isn't usually the type who can easily spend it. They've built their identity around accumulation, around being careful, around always having enough. Even when they have more than enough, that anxiety doesn't just disappear.

The clients who find real happiness in retirement aren't necessarily the wealthiest ones. They're the ones who've figured out something deeper. They wake up with purpose. They contribute to their communities. They mentor young professionals, volunteer at their alma mater, or continue doing work they love because they want to, not because they have to. They've discovered that fulfillment comes not from the size of their portfolio, but from having responsibilities that matter and relationships that endure.

As Justin puts it, money doesn't buy happiness—it buys the time to find it.

WHERE TRADITIONAL FINANCIAL THINKING LETS US DOWN

Most people approach money backwards. They obsess over the mechanics—the budgets, the investment strategies, the tax optimization techniques—without ever asking what it's all for. They master the "how" while ignoring the "why."

This isn't surprising. The financial industry has trained everyone this way. Open any personal finance book and you'll find chapters on compound interest, asset allocation, and withdrawal rates. Important topics, certainly. But when was the last time someone asked what brings you joy? What legacy you want to leave? What dreams you've deferred because you're too busy being practical?

As Taylor likes to remind his clients, real financial planning is more art than science. The most profound conversations in a financial advisor's office rarely start with the rate of return. They start with questions like: "I can retire, but should I?" Or, "We have enough, but enough for what?"

These aren't financial questions at their core. They're human questions. And they require a different framework entirely.

It's time to flip the script on how we think about money.

A DIFFERENT FRAMEWORK: MONEY AS A TOOL FOR LIVING

What if people stopped treating money as the destination and started seeing it as the vehicle?

Over years of sitting with clients through life's biggest decisions, advisors like Taylor and Justin have noticed something profound. The people who use money most wisely don't think about it in terms of accumulation. They think about it in terms of purpose.

The shift changes everything.

Through hundreds of client stories, a pattern emerged. Money serves five fundamental purposes when it's aligned with what matters most: **Living, Changing, Dreaming, Giving, and Enduring**.

These aren't financial categories; they're human ones.

Money is for… LIVING—Understanding when to spend generously and when to save wisely, creating a life of both security and joy.

Money is for… CHANGING—Using money as a tool for successful transitions and avoiding the emotional traps that can turn money into an obstacle during life's inevitable changes.

Money is for… DREAMING—After basic needs are met, money becomes a tool for pursuing your deepest aspirations and most meaningful goals.

Money is for… GIVING—Discovering the profound happiness that comes from generosity, while avoiding the pitfalls of giving with strings attached.

Money is for… ENDURING—Building financial security that lasts and creating legacies that reflect your deepest values.

When you align money with these five purposes, it transforms from an end goal into an enabler of values and aspirations. The focus moves from accumulation to intentional allocation—from hoarding resources to deploying them in service of a meaningful life.

When money becomes a tool for living these five purposes rather than an end in itself, the anxiety that plagues so many successful people begins to fade. The question shifts from "Do I have enough?" to "Am I using what I have in ways that matter?"

THE POWER OF REAL STORIES

Numbers tell us what's possible. Stories show us what's meaningful.

One story in particular continues to evolve, reminding us that our relationship with money is never static.

In the first book, *More Than Money*, Justin shared a story about Ms. Fischer, his 11th-grade teacher, who discovered she could retire ten years earlier than she'd imagined. Thanks to decades of diligent saving and thoughtful investing, she had choices she never thought possible. She sold her Indiana home and headed west to Arizona, ready to embrace the retirement dream of sunshine and leisure.

Life has a way of teaching us what truly matters—often in ways we don't expect.

The dream of living in Arizona had called to Ms. Fischer, and for a time, she answered. She enjoyed her season out west, but through a series of moments and conversations she hadn't planned for, something deeper became clear: her heart still belonged in Indiana.

Rather than let money be the reason she stayed where she no longer felt at home, she chose alignment over attachment. The costs of moving—twice—weren't mistakes. They were part of the process. Part of her learning. And in the end, she could afford to follow what felt right.

Because now, there would be no wondering. No, "What if…?" She had honored the pull, explored the dream, and discovered her truth the only way she could—by living it.

The stories in this book reveal similar moments of clarity— when money stops being the master and becomes the servant of a life well-lived.

You'll meet Linda, who walked away from her high-stress career to hand out tickets at Wrigley Field—discovering that her "retirement failure" was actually her bucket-list dream come true.

You'll follow Rocky and Lu, who made a financial leap to buy 117 acres of wilderness, turning a vacation dream into a 25-year reality.

You'll witness how John's heart attack forced the succession planning he'd avoided for 40 years, as his family grapples with their "third child"—the business.

HOW TO USE THIS BOOK

The pages ahead contain real stories from client families, told by the advisors who walked alongside them through crisis and triumph. Though the names and identifying details have been changed, these aren't case studies or hypotheticals—they're intimate portraits of how money decisions play out in actual human lives.

These stories come from financial advisors in the AGC (Advisors Growing as a Community) network. AGC began with a simple belief: the best advisors don't operate from islands. Members see financial planning as a calling, not just a career, and believe that collaboration makes everyone better. In that spirit, all net proceeds from this book support organizations that offer pro bono financial planning and advance the profession, continuing the cycle of generosity.

The people featured in each story have shared their most intimate financial moments not for recognition, but to light the path for others. Their experiences reveal truths no textbook can teach: that money decisions are really life decisions, that financial plans must bend without breaking, that true wealth has little to do with net worth.

Your guide through these narratives is Justin, who has woven them together with the same care he brings to his own client relationships. He'll help you see the connections between stories, the lessons that transcend individual circumstances, and the wisdom that emerges when people are brave enough to share their truth.

In each section, you'll find not just stories but invitations to reflect. What fears drive your financial decisions? What dreams remain deferred? How might your resources better serve what matters most to you? There are no right answers, only authentic ones.

Use each story to find your own answer to the guiding question:

What is money really for? After years of witnessing clients' struggles and triumphs, the answer is simple but deeply personal. Money is for whatever allows you to live with purpose, navigate change with grace, pursue dreams with courage, give with joy, and create something that endures.

Money isn't just about tomorrow's security—it's about today's meaning. As Justin will show you, "Money isn't just about the future. It's how we experience life right now."

Turn the page. Your journey toward a richer, more intentional life begins now.

MONEY IS FOR...
Living

W HEN WE THINK about saving and investing, we often think of money as a tool for the future. But of course, money isn't just about the future; it's also heavily involved in how we experience life right now.

In the chapters ahead, we embrace the fullness of life as it is—complex, beautiful, messy, and sacred. Here, money is an active participant in our everyday decisions. It shapes how we show up, what we prioritize, and what we say yes to—not someday, but today.

These stories invite us to explore a more human side of finance. They ask deeper questions: What if the best investment isn't in the market, but in peace of mind? What if the purpose of money isn't to retire from life, but to engage more fully with it?

From paying off a mortgage to heal past wounds, to chasing long-postponed adventures, to redefining what "enough" really means, each story reminds us that the goal isn't perfection or maximum return. It's alignment. It's agency. It's a life that feels honest and whole.

Because money well-lived is not about optimizing every dollar—it's about designing a life that makes meaning out of every moment.

WHAT IF TODAY WAS YOUR LAST DAY TO LIVE?

Phil Weiss, CPA, CFA, RLP®
Apprise Wealth Management

LINDA NEVER IMAGINED that handing out tickets at baseball games would be her reality.

But there she was, at 51 years old, wearing her Cubs jersey, surrounded by other ushers who were either half her age or a couple of decades older… having the time of her life.

To outsiders, this might have looked like a "retirement failure"—a woman in her 50s forced to take a low-wage job after a career setback.

But for Linda, her job at Wrigley Field was the fulfillment of a bucket-list dream she'd carried with her since her 20s.

WHY WEALTH DOESN'T EQUAL WELL-BEING

Through my work as a Financial Life Planner, I've learned that dreams aren't always what society tells us they should be.

We're conditioned to chase impressive retirements, luxury vacations, and exclusive club memberships. We measure success by the size of our investment accounts.

Linda had all that—a successful career, substantial savings, and a clear path to a secure, abundant retirement.

On paper, she was thriving.

But a few years into our planning relationship, Linda started to feel like something was off. Pretty soon, she confessed to me that she was "drowning in stress."

She'd been working nonstop for 35 years since the age of 14. She was managing a high-pressure job, two teenage daughters, four properties, and her mother's financial affairs after her mom received an Alzheimer's diagnosis.

After months of carrying too much, Linda decided to take 12 weeks of family leave from her job to de-stress, get her bearings, and re-evaluate her options.

As she started thinking about what lay ahead, Linda reached out to me with a question: "What if I don't go back to work?"

What she was really asking was more profound: "What kind of life do I want to be living?"

Not long after, we agreed to work on her life plan. A little later on, I received an email from Linda.

During some free time, she had read my life plan, which was posted on my firm's website. I've posted my life plan there for two reasons:

1. I ask clients to share a lot when we work on their life plans, so I feel it's only right for me to share mine.
2. I hope reading my life plan will inspire others to go through the process openly.

Reading my life plan helped Linda realize she had been chasing the wrong idea of success. Up to this point, she had been trying to save "enough" money to retire without defining what "enough" really meant.

Now, she understood that to have "enough," she needed to clearly define what kind of life she wanted to live.

This shift gave her a new lens. It wasn't about chasing more money but about creating more meaning in her life.

THE POWER OF A LIFE PLAN

When Linda told me she was considering leaving her high-stress job, we went back to the drawing board and started working on her life plan. I asked her a question I always ask clients when we work on their life plans.

"If your doctor told you that this was your last day to live, what did you not get to do? Who did you not get to be? What did you miss?"

Linda's answers didn't come to her immediately. But she knew that "saving more" or "being wealthier" weren't up there at all.

Traditional financial planning often focuses solely on the numbers and wealth accumulation—building the biggest pile of money possible, all in the name of security.

Sure, it includes goals, but most of them are numbers-based. Money is a tool, however, not a goal. If we understand this, we can use it more effectively to achieve our desired outcomes and live a more fulfilling life.

In other words, the traditional approach misses the central question: What is this money for?

Linda already had enough money (even if she didn't realize it yet). What she didn't have was enough life—especially enough time for life due to her demanding career.

Time is the one resource we can't get more of, but the relationship between money and time can't be ignored. Most of us spend our working years trading our time for money. But we can also use our money to buy back time for ourselves.

REDEFINING ENOUGH

Linda's financial journey had started early. When she graduated from college, her father gave her an invaluable gift—a brokerage account with a modest amount to invest.

This gift sparked her interest in investing and gave her a head start many don't receive. She'd built on that foundation expertly, but somewhere along the way, the means had become the end.

Now that Linda was questioning what was next for her, we needed to reframe her relationship with money. Instead of viewing it as something to accumulate, she could see money as a tool for creating the life she truly wanted.

Together, we explored what "enough" meant for her. Not in terms of a specific dollar amount—she'd been there, done that. She was already stuck in a cycle familiar to many successful people: hitting financial milestones, then immediately setting higher ones without stopping to ask why or how much she truly needed.

Through our conversations, we identified what actually mattered to her: time with her daughters as they transitioned to adulthood, more time with her husband, Steve, less stress, more joy in her daily life, and more time to take care of herself.

BEYOND THE NUMBERS

When we discussed potential obstacles standing in her way, financial concerns naturally arose.

Could she really afford to leave her career? What about their retirement plans? Their plans to travel to exotic places? Their daughters' college funds? Would their future still feel secure?

This is where financial knowledge is crucial. We revisited Linda and Steve's financial plan. The numbers confirmed what I suspected: They were already saving more than they needed.

With Steve's income, they could maintain their lifestyle. Their retirement was still on track. Their daughters' educations were funded.

Ultimately, Linda's biggest obstacle wasn't financial. It was her mindset and the work she would need to do to reimagine her identity. After decades of a successful career, Linda feared she might not know who she was anymore if she stopped working.

She also feared judgment from others who might see her choice as a step backward, or would question how she could stop working. Linda and Steve do not live lavishly. They don't drive fancy cars. Very few people know much about their true financial position.

Because this is difficult work, I encouraged Linda to remember why she had started saving and investing so much in the first place: to give her freedom.

At times, Linda needed a reminder that she was fortunate to be where she was financially. She only needed to give herself permission to take advantage of the freedom she had earned.

A DREAM REIMAGINED

About a year after we started our life planning sessions, Linda shared something unexpected with me.

She sent me an email explaining that back in her 20s, she had a bucket-list dream while at a Cubs game. Not working as an executive. Not watching from a luxury suite. Just handing out tickets or working as an usher like the "little old ladies" she saw doing that job.

She went online and found a job posting. She applied and received a link to schedule an interview two days later.

On the day of the interview, Linda showed up in her Cubs jersey, tastefully layered over her World Series T-shirt. The other applicants—mostly college students in business-casual attire—stared at her a little curiously.

But Linda wasn't there to impress anyone with corporate polish. She was there to fulfill a dream.

Spoiler: She got the job.

I was so excited when she told me. Years ago, I'd worked a spring job at a stadium, too. It was just for fun—handing out programs, helping fans find their seats—but I remembered how much I'd enjoyed the energy and excitement. I knew exactly why this seemingly simple job could mean so much to her.

"I'm not sure I'll last the whole season," she told me. "I might be crazy for trying—but I'm excited. I at least want to make it through the big concert this summer."

WHEN JOY MATTERS MORE THAN MONEY

Well, Linda made it through the whole season—and had a blast. She even worked at the Winter Classic hockey game, held at Wrigley Field on December 31.

Sure, the pay didn't move the needle.

But the experience? It was priceless. She worked games and events, met new people, and made memories. She was also assigned to take care of some first-time attendees at the park.

Wrigley is an iconic ballpark. She got to take advantage of the full experience and help others enjoy it, too.

(And no, the Cubs didn't win the World Series, so no replica ring. But that didn't stop her from having a great time.) She has many stories to share about the crazy things she did the year after she retired from her corporate job.

Not many of us get that chance.

THE DEEPER REWARD

Linda's life today looks very different from how it did before. She's still busy, but in a new way. Her time is now spent on things and experiences that bring her joy and fulfillment. She's more relaxed. Less stressed. She's present with both her family and herself.

My favorite part of the life planning process is the opportunity it provides to truly get to know clients and what matters most to them.

In fact, Linda is more than a client to me. We've grown close. Our meetings always include time to talk about life, not just finances, and she often schedules extra time with me, so we don't have to rush those conversations.

She even invited me to fly out and meet some of her friends. I did, and I was honored. I arrived a day early so we could attend the local St. Patrick's Day parade. Linda wanted more of her friends to see and understand the benefits of life planning and working with a financial advisor.

During that meeting, Linda told her friends that working with me on her life plan changed her life.

Later, she and her family visited my area, and we met in person again for brunch. Our spouses and one of Linda's daughters joined us.

We no longer have just an advisor and client relationship. We're friends.

Linda knows I have her back. Whenever anything related to her or her family's finances happens, Linda reaches out to me. I've met her father on Zoom and helped with estate planning issues. Currently, her brother is facing a major health scare. Linda has also asked for my help in understanding and managing his finances.

I'm honored to be a trusted resource for Linda and her family.

A LIFE TRANSFORMED

Ultimately, Linda didn't need to chase more money. She needed to give herself permission to pursue more meaning.

It all started with a simple shift from asking, "Do I have enough?" to "What kind of life do I want to live?"

She made that shift. She stepped off the treadmill. She started living life on her terms.

And she's happier because of it.

For Linda, the joy wasn't in retiring early—but finally living intentionally.

Now, if a doctor were ever to tell Linda she had one day left to live, she'd be able to say proudly that she'd fulfilled her young adult dream of working at the Cubs stadium.

And she'd had a grand old time doing it.

FINAL THOUGHTS

You may have enough money. But do you have enough life?

Ask yourself the question Linda did—the one that changed everything for her:

What kind of life do I want to live?

The answer might change your life, too.

REFLECTIVE QUESTIONS

- What kind of life do I want to live?
- You may have enough money. But do you have enough life?

———————

This content is for informational and educational purposes only and does not constitute financial, legal, or tax advice. Phil Weiss is the Principal and Founder of Apprise Wealth Management, a registered investment adviser.

THE JOURNEY FROM FINANCIAL PASSIVITY TO A LIFE OF ADVENTURE

Jared Tanimoto, CFP®
Sedai Wealth

W HAT DOES A life of adventure mean to you? Sailing across the Pacific? Visiting the Pyramids? Perhaps, for you, it's simply a quiet cabin in the woods? For one client of mine, it was living the van life.

When Jim first sat down in my office, he was polite and friendly, but a bit skeptical.

"I don't even know if I'm in the right place," he admitted. "I'm not even close to being retired, but I read that I should be investing. I have these old stock options from my last job, I don't know how much they're worth—if anything. Compound interest sounds great in theory, but it feels like a scam. Right?"

THE CASH HOARDING ENGINEER

Like many millennials, when Jim had questions about life hacks, he dove headfirst into online forums searching for answers. After multiple Reddit thread rabbit-holes about the best ways to make, save, and invest money, he grew overwhelmed by the conflicting information. Some said the stock market was a racket, a way for the rich to get even richer. Other folks raved about compound interest. Get in now, they advised, while you're still young and have plenty of time.

"I have decent savings," he added. "But now I'm wondering if it's just sitting around losing value thanks to inflation." He sighed and slumped in his chair. "I'm just not the kinda guy who makes risky moves. I could lose everything I've worked so hard for."

I leaned forward and smiled to ease his anxiety. "What do you want your money to do for you?" I asked.

"Do for me?" he replied.

"Yeah," I picked up a photo of me with my family at Zion National Park. "I like traveling to places where I can backpack or mountain bike. And thanks to smart financial planning, I can afford to take my wife and kids on these trips."

"Must be nice," Jim responded.

"What inspires and motivates you?" I asked. "Tell me about your life goals. I can guarantee your financial goals are intertwined with these. What makes Jim tick?"

His face lit up for a moment, but then he dropped his head and gave an embarrassed laugh.

"Technically, I'm a software engineer," he said. "But the other day my boss caught me watching YouTube videos. Van life stuff. He was not amused."

"It's not that I hate my job," he continued. "I make good money. But lately it doesn't feel like enough. You know, I realized I spend more than half my waking hours in the same office, at the same desk, and grabbing the same cup of coffee at the same cafe every morning."

The spark in his eyes returned. "In my free time, though, I surf through videos of van lifers thinking about how cool it would be driving across the country spending my days rock climbing in as many of the 63 National Parks as possible. That's pretty crazy, right?"

I could relate. Jim would be considered successful by traditional standards. Six-figure salary with benefits, check. Nice condo, check. Bills covered, check. A few nights out on the town here and there, well, when he allowed for it in his budget. But, night after night, he scrolled through TikTok, Instagram, and YouTube watching adventure content creators do their thing.

"Jared," he sounded almost desperate, "there are people out there exploring every day, rock climbing as often as they want, and they're making money doing it! In 20 years, hell, even in five or ten years, I have no idea where I'll be, and I don't want to regret my decisions."

Jim wasn't a rare case. Sometimes after people get what they think they always wanted—in his case the stability and predictability of being a software engineer—they realize it's not what they wanted at all, but they're too scared to make any moves that might jeopardize their financial security.

He thought he should be content and grateful. He got himself through college debt-free. He received a job offer soon after graduating and settled into corporate life. But whenever he ached to do something different or break outside the box, his self-doubt held him back. His old thoughts would play on repeat: don't quit a good job, save your money, stay out of debt.

JIM'S MONEY MINDSET SHIFT

Despite his success, Jim found himself hoarding every dollar. A van would cost money, upkeep would cost money, growing channel fans would take a lot of time. His old money habits and beliefs had kept him scared and stuck for far too long.

"So," I said, "it's not that you don't have any money, it's that you don't feel safe using it on anything frivolous?"

"Yeah," he said. "I guess that's about it."

I explained to Jim that investing isn't gambling—it's strategic risk-taking. "Just like rock climbing," I pointed out. "You don't just throw yourself off a cliff—you plan your climb, use the right gear, and make smart moves. If you understand when it's appropriate to take more risks—like when you have decades until retirement—you can manage investments more effectively."

We talked about different strategies and tools he could use based on his personal financial goals. What resonated most for him was something called The Bucket Strategy, a way of dividing money into different "climbs" according to one's financial timelines.

I could practically hear the wheels turning in his head, and all the pieces clicking into place. Jim realized investing could empower him, not entrap him.

We scheduled our next meeting—his stride much lighter as he left.

CHOOSING ADVENTURE OVER COMFORT

Once Jim figured out how investing and compound interest actually work, he re-examined his life, excited about the possibilities.

Over the next few months, we worked together to create a financial plan that allowed him to explore his lifelong dream of travel and adventure, without jeopardizing his long-term security. We also dug into those stock options and, turns out, Jim already had a good chunk of change invested. We decided to move the bulk of his cash, and his company stock options, into a strategic, diversified portfolio based on his goals. The remainder he used as his startup funds.

After years of sitting on the sidelines while his favorite creators blew up the internet, Jim finally took a risk on himself. His budgeted startup funds could float him for months—maybe even years, with some part-time contracting work.

He rented his condo, sold his sedan, and bought a used, full-size 2019 Ford Transit. Over the next 11 weeks, he converted it into the campervan of his dreams. He documented the entire process for his YouTube channel and gained hundreds of paid subscribers before he'd even embarked on his first big rock-climbing trip—Yosemite National Park.

With his financial game set, Jim resigned from his job and jumped into life as a full-time content creator, growing his following at a faster pace than he'd ever had time to do before. His gamble on himself paid off. He would never again allow his money to fester away, devalued by inflation. Instead, he took advantage of his age and early financial success to build wealth for himself through smart investments.

Yes, he was nervous at first, but all it took was some understanding of the stock market, the different types of asset classes, and the risks associated with each one so he could make informed decisions. Knowledge is financial power. Jim now understands the purpose of investing in long-term growth, not short-term gains, and that long and steady gives him the security to balance his life with play today.

That security also allows Jim to not get caught up in the day-to-day market fluctuations. Investing doesn't have to wreak havoc with your nervous system. Getting over his fear of running out of money wasn't easy, but it was worth it. I could see it on his face when he stopped by my office on his way to Yosemite to say goodbye and thank you.

And to make sure I had his YouTube channel link.

THE REWARDS OF TAKING ACTION

Today, Jim thrives out on the open road, despite stepping away from his "safe" career path. He returns home now and then to visit family and take a break from van life, but he couldn't be happier. He's been out on the road for two years and has visited ten National Parks. His audience keeps growing, month after month, allowing him to continue earning money while doing exactly what he loves.

Beyond the joy his new career brings, Jim has peace of mind around money. He leverages YouTube ads and brand partnerships for steady income. He maintains a decent level of cash savings for emergencies and puts a good portion of his income towards investments each month. He checks in on his investments quarterly as his accounts continue to grow.

IN SUMMARY

Inaction is riskier because when it comes to investing, time is your most valuable asset.

If you feel stuck, ask yourself: Am I working for money, or is money working for me?

Investing helps combat inflation. It makes the difference between standing still financially and reaching your wealth goals.

Knowing how to save money is important, but it's also valuable to know how and when to spend it.

Investing doesn't have to be all or nothing. You can start small. The most important part is to start now.

Financial planning isn't just for your retirement. It's for building a life that excites you—now and in the future.

REFLECTIVE QUESTIONS

- What experiences would I regret not pursuing if I looked back ten or 20 years from now?
- If money was no longer a limiting factor, what is one thing I would do differently right now?
- How do I define a "rich life" beyond my bank account balance?

BEYOND THE BALANCE SHEET: THE HUMAN SIDE OF MONEY

Cody Murray, MBA, CFP®
Stillwater Financial Services

MINDY WAS SHY and hesitant to talk during our first few meetings, but when she did open up, everything changed.

Her husband, Mark, reached out months before inquiring about financial planning. Naturally, he led the discussions and answered most of the questions. Mark was a few years into starting and running his medical practice. He arrived at a common place in a business owner's journey when the business was just recently profitable, and cash was starting to build up. He didn't know what to do next. Should I pay down debt? Invest? If so, how or in which account? These questions and many more prompted Mark to reach out and begin the financial planning process.

The first meeting was pretty typical. We reviewed his balance sheet, talked about his practice, and listed out his goals and ideas for his money. Mark was driven by his vision and desire to build and accumulate wealth. He had plans for a second location, buying real estate with the use of debt, and investing in a new 401(k). With Mindy's income of $90,000 along with Mark's income of $150,000, the couple had lots of savings potential which Mark gladly allocated to achieve his goals.

When guiding a client through the financial planning process, planners use goals to "begin with the end in mind," as Stephen Covey used to say. Meaning, if Mark had a goal of building a real estate portfolio, and he wants to start by purchasing a $500,000 rental property, we would work to save up for the $100,000 down payment. If Mark and Mindy had $5,000 to save every month, the plan would be to save $5,000 for around 20 months in order to buy the property. Oftentimes, clients have several financial goals that compete for their "extra dollars," so prioritization is required.

Mark was focused on wealth accumulation, and therefore, every eligible dollar was assigned to an investment. Mindy was supportive of all of these ideas and the general direction of the plan; she also wanted to grow the family's wealth. However, I could tell she wasn't as engaged as I thought she should be. Fortunately, the second meeting in our process was designed to uncover the deeper meaning of money and our relationship with it. I give all credit to Carl Richards who shared this line of questioning with me. Here is how the meeting went:

Cody: "To start off I'd like to ask you both an unusual question. If you two were out to dinner with another couple, which one of you would do most of the talking?"

Mark and Mindy both pointed to Mark.

Cody: "Ok, thanks, this is great. In that case, I'll start by asking Mindy a few questions first. Is that ok with you all?"

Mindy reluctantly agrees.

Cody: "Mindy, can you tell me why money is important to you."

Mindy: "Money provides security and freedom."

(In my years of experience, security and freedom are the most common answers given.)

Cody: "Security and freedom can mean a lot of different things to people. Can you tell me what they look like for you?"

Mindy: "Just the ability to do what I want when I want to. Like travel and have nice things."

(Once again these are very common answers.)

At this moment I can see words start to build up in Mark's eyes. He wants to chime in so bad, but I hold him off and ask one more question.

Cody: "How about this, tell me about a time when you didn't feel financially secure."

Mindy, after looking at Mark: "Probably right when we got married and Mark had just started his practice and I was new at my job."

Cody: "Ok, so your budget was probably tight or maybe even negative and you might not have had much money in the bank."

Mindy: "Yes, exactly. The practice was a big risk, and it wasn't clear if it was going to work. Those were stressful months."

Cody: "Ok thanks for sharing. Mark, it's your turn... Same questions: Why is money so important to you?"

Mark: "Is it ok if I add to Mindy's answer?"

Cody: "Well, If Mindy is ok with it. Those were her answers."

Mindy knew what was coming and finally caved. She nodded and Mark continued.

Mark: "Mindy and her mom spent most of her childhood homeless. Not in the traditional sense, where they were living on the street, but more like housing insecurity. They would couch-hop, or sleep in family and friends' garages or spare rooms. Sometimes, they would get an apartment for a few weeks, but they never spent long in any place."

Cody: "Mindy, is that about right? How do you think that experience affects your view of money now?"

Mindy: "Yes, that's about it. I don't really know. I try not to think about it. I just know I'm in a better place."

Cody: "Let's take a step back and talk about how money can provide security for you, Mindy. Maybe something related to your childhood experience."

Mindy: "I can tell you I don't like moving. I love our house and it's big enough to raise our kids."

Cody: "How can money help you not have to worry about moving again?"

Mindy: "I suppose if it was paid off, I wouldn't need to worry. (Pause.) Then nobody could ever tell us we had to leave."

Sometimes, hearing yourself say something hits deeper. The idea of creating her own housing or financial security by paying off her house never crossed her mind, but when she heard herself say it, her past financial trauma seemed to find its remedy. At that moment, I could tell this was more than money. It was about living.

"Sometimes the greatest investment you can make is paying down debt and achieving emotional peace."
—David Bach, *The Automatic Millionaire*

For Mindy, housing insecurity haunted her into adulthood despite having ample financial resources. Most of the time debt reduction, especially low-interest loans like home mortgages, is less about the money and more about the emotion.

Morgan Housel, author of *The Psychology of Money*, said this about paying off your mortgage: "On paper, it's the dumbest thing you could possibly do. Even though it's the worst financial decision we've ever made, I think it's the best money decision we've ever made. It's one thing that gives us a level of independence and autonomy."

Morgan continued: "People should not just aim to be rational on a spreadsheet—rational on paper, I think, is not a good financial goal. People should aim to be reasonable and manage their own financial decisions about what makes them happy, and what helps them sleep at night."

The point isn't that debt is bad and needs to be paid off. Although I think it should be. The point I want to make is that people's financial decisions are about what makes them happy, and what helps them sleep at night. It's about living.

We went on to prioritize paying off their house debt along with a few small saving goals, like investing, as a part of their financial plan. Now, years later, and after paying off their home, Mark and Mindy feel free to live their best lives.

Mark and Mindy, along with their kids, travel frequently and have been able to pivot to their other financial goals, such as investing. Although they postponed investing and saving while they paid off their home, they made it work and have no regrets. In their case, paying off their home debt was a source of major financial stress. For others it could be saving for their kids' education or having a large cash reserve. Regardless of the financial goal, your money should work to make your life better.

FINAL THOUGHTS

- Identifying financial hardships can help you understand how money affects you.
- Talking about money with another person can help you discover some of your financial blind spots.
- Balancing qualitative goals like debt reduction and quantitative financial goals can lead to a more fulfilling financial future.

REFLECTIVE QUESTIONS

- What experiences from your past might be quietly influencing your current relationship with money?
- If you had to choose between what looks best "on the spreadsheet" versus what would help you sleep better at night, which financial decision would you make differently?
- How do you and your partner (if applicable) really define financial security and freedom—beyond the surface-level answers?

———

THE ILLUSION OF "ENOUGH"

Rebecca Jackson, CFP®, CPA/PFS, RLP®
SeedSafe Financial LLC

BILL STARED AT the screen, heart pounding. The stock price had hit his dream number—the number we'd calculated as his level for financial freedom. But instead of selling, he hesitated. Maybe it would go even higher, he thought.

Six months later, it was down 90%.

I've worked with Bill's family for eight years. They embody a quiet wealth mindset—grateful, frugal, and deeply rooted in their values. This approach had served them well, but nothing could have prepared them for the biggest financial ride of their lives.

Bill and his wife, Sarah, lived in a modest three-bedroom home in a quiet LA suburb. Their weekends were filled with soccer games, family time, and volunteering at their kids' schools. Sarah was a therapist, and while they didn't have excess money, they always found ways to make things work. Hand-me-downs, DIY home repairs, and a strict grocery budget were part of their everyday routine.

"We're lucky," Sarah often said, the epitome of optimism and contentment. "We have everything we need."

Bill was an engineer and took a more quantitative approach to life. He was a founding team member of a startup and advanced his career to Principal Engineer—enjoying diving into the code and coaching other engineers. When the company was acquired by a private firm preparing for an IPO, his workload became relentless.

There was no more time to coach engineers—the work had to be done immediately. Tasks piled up and the long hours drained him. When he came to me, he was exhausted, ready for a way out.

"I just want to be done," he told me. "I want this IPO to be my way to never work again."

"If you could wave a magic wand, what would your ideal life look like?" I asked.

We mapped it out—dreaming, estimating costs, and defining the financial milestones that would give him security, comfort, and, ultimately, the freedom to own his time.

THE IPO WINDFALL—OR SO IT SEEMED

Bill's family had always been careful with money. They clipped coupons, rarely splurged, and found joy in their children and community. While they didn't have much to give financially, they shared their time and talents generously. They felt content with what they had, grateful for the relationships that enriched their lives.

Then came the IPO.

As the stock price climbed, they cautiously embraced a few luxuries. Bill bought a new car, his wife left her job, and they began to spend more freely. As soon as Bill could start selling shares, we took a little off the table to create some financial security.

Then, it happened.

The stock price popped.

He had reached the number that meant he never had to work again. But when it was time to sell, he hesitated.

"What if it goes even higher?" he wondered.

He had more money on paper than ever before, yet it didn't feel like enough.

They upgraded to a bigger home. They traveled more. They already felt financially free—so why sell?

For six months, I heard these kinds of statements from Bill:

"I know I should sell, but what if it doubles?"

"Look how much it's gone up already. It'll keep climbing."

"My coworkers are still holding—if they're not worried, why should I be?"

"If I sell, I'll have to pay taxes. I'll just wait until next year."

"This company is different. It's a game-changer."

Then, as quickly as it had risen, the stock crashed.

At first, he told himself it was temporary.

"It's just a dip," Bill reassured himself.

The next week, down another 20%. Then 30%.

"It'll bounce back," he said.

But it didn't.

The stock price fell over 90%—and stayed there.

His dream of financial freedom slipped through his fingers.

REGRET, REFLECTION, AND A NEW DEFINITION OF WEALTH

For months, Bill wrestled with regret. If only I had sold. If only I had been smarter. He replayed every decision, every moment of hesitation. But then, one day, he came to me with a different perspective.

"I used to think money was the goal," he said. "Now, I see it's just a tool. And we're using it to build a life we love."

Before the IPO, his life had been about saving, saving, saving— but at what cost? He had been so focused on securing the future that he wasn't fully living in the present.

The IPO didn't give him the wealth to walk away from work, but it gave him something else: a new understanding of wealth.

Bill and his family still had financial security. And now, instead of obsessing over growing their net worth, they leaned into what truly made them happy—traveling together, spending time with their community, and giving back in meaningful ways.

He didn't have as much money as he once did.

But for the first time in his life, he felt rich.

REFLECTIVE QUESTIONS

- What stories do I tell myself about "missing out"? How do they influence my decisions?
- What is *my number*—the amount I believe will make me feel free—and why that number?
- What role does humility play in my financial journey? What has it taught me?

———————

The above discussion is for informational purposes only. Recommendations are of a general nature, not based on knowledge of any individual's specific needs or circumstances, and there is no intent to provide individual investment advisory, supervisory, or management services.

SUMMARY OF
MONEY IS FOR...
Living

L IVING A FULFILLED life isn't about having the most—it's about making the most of what you have.

In this first section, we've seen that money isn't just for growing or saving. It's for experiencing. For creating peace of mind. For taking chances. For feeling alive. Whether it's paying off a home to heal old wounds, hitting the road to chase a dream, trading titles for joy, or learning the hard way what enough really means, each story reminds us that financial planning is ultimately life planning.

The best use of money is to make life better, not later, but now.

Because living a fulfilled life isn't what happens after the plan works out. It's what you can experience along the way when you design your financial life around your own goals and values.

DESIGN YOUR FINANCIAL LIFE: MONEY IS FOR... *Living*

Start with life, not numbers
☐ Before chasing more, ask: What kind of life feels whole, alive, and meaningful to me? Build your vision from there.

Define "Enough" in every dimension
☐ Enough isn't a number—it's a feeling. What helps you feel safe, content, and free? Emotionally. Spiritually. Relationally. Financially.

Come home to the present
☐ It's easy to get caught up chasing the next goal or milestone. But what if you paused and asked yourself: *What already brings me joy, peace, and a sense of aliveness today?* You might discover that you're closer to "enough" than you ever realized.

Notice what you're trading
☐ What are you giving up due to your current spending? Time, health, presence, joy—what are you spending to accumulate?
☐ Is your spending aligned with your values?

Reclaim your real wealth

☐ Your time, energy, attention, and relationships represent your most valued assets. Are you investing them in the life you want to be living?

Live like time matters

☐ If tomorrow were your last day, what would you regret not having done? Let that truth guide your next step.

MONEY IS FOR...
Changing

I N MANY AREAS of our lives the thought of change might make us uncomfortable, even scared. But it's often in these times of uncertainty where we discover deeper truths and strengths about ourselves.

This section is about transformation, not just financial but personal. It's also about the moments when something shifts—a job ends, a dream evolves, a belief breaks open—and we're left to ask ourselves: Who am I now? And how can my money support the person I'm becoming?

The following stories reveal how money can be more than a source of stability—it can be an instrument of renewal. Sometimes that means stepping away from a life that no longer fits. Sometimes it means embracing a new identity, a new purpose, or a new path forward. And sometimes, it means doing the deep work of letting go—of fear, of past mistakes, of stories we've long outgrown.

Money can't protect us from change. But it can help us move through it with courage and clarity. It can give us the freedom to pause, pivot, heal, and begin again.

Because the point of planning isn't just to stay the course—it's to have the flexibility to change course when your heart says it's time.

I'M JUST A POOR WIDOW

Greg Kurinec, CFP®
Pennant Planning

When life changes dramatically, money becomes a powerful tool not just for survival, but also for creating a meaningful new chapter.

IT'S A BITTER January morning in suburban Chicago. A fresh, heavy snow has buried the neighborhood. Jeanne, bundled in thick winter gear, stands at the edge of her garage, shovel in hand. Her driveway stretches out before her—long, frozen, and untouched. She has an exercise class to attend, something small but important—a routine that helps her feel normal again. But before she can leave the house, she has to clear a path herself. There's no one else to do it. Not anymore.

When Jeanne lost John, her husband of 55 years, the world turned upside down. They had been high school sweethearts, building a life together through decades of raising four children, moving for John's career at DuPont, and eventually settling into a comfortable retirement.

John had always handled finances, balancing the checkbook, investing in stocks, and managing taxes. Jeanne ran the home with grace and devotion.

For John, managing their finances wasn't a chore, it was a passion.

He treated it like a hobby, poring over market news, researching investment options, and carefully tending to their portfolio.

Jeanne never felt the need to get involved. She trusted him implicitly. Finances were his domain, and she gave him the space to enjoy it. She always came along to meetings with their financial advisor, sitting quietly beside him, listening while John asked the questions and steered the conversation. She was grateful to be included, but she was perfectly content in the background, confident that John had it all under control.

In the first days after John's funeral, Jeanne moved through a fog of condolences, casseroles, and paperwork. Somewhere between changing the name on the bank accounts and canceling John's subscriptions, a creeping fear took hold. She almost felt like she was erasing him. Every bill that arrived felt like a threat. Every unknown envelope seemed to reinforce that she was now on her own. There was always this doubt in the back of her mind: "Is this what John would do?" Was she unraveling a lifetime of well-thought-out decisions? There were moments she felt paralyzed by the fear of making a mistake.

"I'm just a poor widow," Jeanne muttered often, sometimes to herself, sometimes to her children when they offered to help. These words shielded her against the overwhelming reality that she didn't know if she could afford the life she and John had built together.

Jeanne worried about spending on things that she and John had never done before. This fear drove her to do things like shoveling heavy snow, laying mulch, and maintaining the home as if John were still around. Deep down, she knew she shouldn't be doing these things, but she thought that every dollar saved would mean that she would be alright.

One of Jeanne's biggest fears was running out of money. She remembered the struggles she and John went through early in their marriage with four kids—pinching pennies to ensure there would be a warm meal on the table. She didn't want to go back to those days, or worse, become a burden on her children.

After most of the dust had settled, Jeanne finally decided it was time to meet with Greg, the family's longtime financial advisor. John had been the one who understood investments, Medicare, and taxes. She felt that she owed it to him to hear Greg out and continue the relationship. Jeanne was nervous going in but thought, what was left for her to do to but tighten her belt and hope for the best?

In Greg's office, Jeanne sat stiffly in the chair, a heavy folder clutched in her lap—its seams strained by weeks of unopened mail. The weight of it wasn't just paper; it was everything she didn't yet understand. Greg's voice was calm and steady, a kind presence in the storm.

He assured her that John had done well, planned carefully, and invested wisely. Jeanne had always believed that, deep down. But hearing it spoken aloud, by someone who knew the numbers, gave her a comfort she hadn't expected.

Greg explained there would be a lot to sort through, but they'd go at her pace—there was no rush, no pressure. Just one step at a time. That first meeting wasn't about strategies or decisions. It was simply about opening the folder, sorting the mail, and breathing through it all. For Jeanne, slow and steady was more than a rhythm. It was the only way forward.

In subsequent meetings, Greg explained that she would move from filing jointly to filing singly, which would increase her taxes. Medicare premiums would also rise, although they could appeal.

He mentioned investments; stocks John had chosen carefully over decades. Amazon, Greg noted, had performed exceptionally well. Jeanne had heard John talk about Amazon before and knew her grandkids were using it all the time, but she had no idea about any of the particulars.

As Greg began to go into more depth on the Amazon holding, Jeanne developed a sense of pride. It was her husband who picked this stock and created this great wealth because of it. That also made it all the more difficult to part with it. She was not yet ready to let go of the stock. She was not ready to let go of John.

Despite Greg's steady tone and encouraging words, deep down, Jeanne felt a sense of panic. Taxes going up. Medicare costs rising. Stocks she didn't understand.

"I'm a poor widow," she repeated aloud. "How am I going to afford this?"

Greg paused, hands folded. "Jeanne," he said gently, "you're not poor. You're in a good place. But we'll take this one step at a time. We are going to move at your pace." It wasn't something she could absorb all at once. The fear was too ingrained. John had been her protector. Now she felt unprotected and exposed.

The first few months were hard. Jeanne found herself fretting over small expenses: the leaking faucet she didn't know how to fix, the rising heating bill, the property tax bill. Every decision felt like she was approaching the edge of a cliff.

At first, Jeanne waited for Greg's calls. She never initiated. It seemed too bold, too risky—what if she asked the wrong question?

But gradually, something shifted. After a confusing letter from Medicare, she picked up the phone. Greg talked her through the appeal process. At first, she was wary but knew what had to be done. She needed to take ownership.

A few weeks later, she won the appeal. Her premium stayed lower. A small victory, but one that planted a seed of confidence. For the first time in her life, she had a financial win all by herself. This provided the momentum she needed to begin to tackle the rest.

Next came the investments. Jeanne learned, slowly, that she didn't have to sell all the stocks John had picked. Some she could hold. Some she could trim to provide cash flow. She didn't have to understand every market detail, only enough to make informed choices.

By the end of the year, Jeanne was no longer waiting passively. She scheduled her own meetings with Greg. She kept a notebook of questions. She even found herself smiling when she talked about finances, a far cry from the fear that had paralyzed her months before.

Believe it or not, Jeanne even called to initiate a conversation about the Amazon stock. This caught Greg off guard. He thought for sure this was something Jeanne would hold onto forever.

She had seen all over the news how it was hitting all-time highs day after day. She wanted to know what would happen if she decided to sell. They discussed the tax implications, increased Medicare premiums, and overall portfolio impact. After going through all of the implications, Jeanne nodded her head and said, "I think it's time."

There was a small part of Jeanne that was sad to let Amazon go. John had built a great legacy for their family with his wise investment, but she also knew that if he were still alive, he would not hesitate to make the decision to exit if he knew the time was right.

One day, sitting at her kitchen table reviewing her accounts, Jeanne looked out the window and thought about her grandchildren. College tuition loomed for the older ones. Summer camps, music lessons, braces for the younger ones.

John had always talked about leaving a legacy. Jeanne realized, with a bittersweet smile, that the legacy wasn't just money sitting quietly in an account. It was life, growing and unfolding, right in front of her.

She didn't need to hoard every penny out of fear. She could use her resources to make a difference now.

The first check she wrote was to a lawn care company. She no longer had to worry about who was going to cut the grass and shovel the snow. This was something she could now take off her plate completely. A sense of relief washed over her. This also made her family very happy. They had worried about their mother doing these back breaking chores.

In the months that followed, she helped where it mattered most. She covered the cost of summer programs, surprised her daughter with a new set of tires when she needed them, and hired help to maintain the big family home. This allowed Jeanne to stay there longer, hosting birthdays and holidays just as she always had.

By quietly stepping in to help the family when they needed it, Jeanne found herself merging the roles she and John had once held separately. It felt meaningful to support her children and grandchildren in new ways, different from the hands-on caregiving of their younger years.

Now, she was helping with tuition checks, unexpected expenses, or small acts of generosity that carried great weight. And in doing so, she was stepping into John's shoes—not by mimicking his every move, but by becoming the family's financial steward in her own quiet, thoughtful way.

Each act of giving chipped away at the "poor widow" image she had carried. She was not poor. She was not powerless. She was a guardian for what she and John had built together, and she had the wisdom now to do it well.

The next Thanksgiving, the entire family gathered at Jeanne's house, the kitchen filled with the chaotic joy of grandchildren, laughter, and the smell of turkey roasting. As she sat in her favorite chair, watching her family orbit around her, Jeanne felt a swell of gratitude and pride.

Jeanne now knows that she will be able to stay in her home for as long as she wishes. The obstacles that might have forced her to leave have been overcome by her confidence that she will be alright. Jeanne misses John every day but is so thankful for the stewardship he provided throughout their marriage.

Looking out her window on a winter morning, Jeanne watches a snowplow clear her driveway—a service she now happily pays for. She smiles, remembering how she once stood there with a shovel, not just clearing snow but also holding tight to every penny out of fear.

There are times when she will still call herself a "poor widow," but now it's said playfully with a nod and wink to those early days. Deep down, Jeanne knows that she is on solid ground, and it is now her turn to be a steward of their wealth.

Jeanne's relationship with money evolved from her early days sitting quietly in the office chair next to John, through the paralysis she felt soon after John passed, to now thriving and having confidence in each financial decision she makes.

She had changed. She had met adversity with action. Money was no longer something to cling to tightly in fear, but something to use. Not just for surviving—but for living.

Money is for changing—changing lives, changing futures, and changing your own story.

REFLECTIVE QUESTIONS

- How might your relationship with money change during major life transitions?
- What financial beliefs might be limiting your ability to adapt to new circumstances?
- Are you using money as a tool for meaningful change, or simply preserving it out of habit or fear?

WHEN IT RAINS,
IT POURS

Yohance Harrison, BFA™, CRPC®
Money Script Wealth Management

S TELLA HAD FINALLY made it—at least, she thought she had. After slogging through college, medical school, and residency, she was finally an attending emergency physician. Yet, this first role in her dream career did not bring her the financial and personal satisfaction she expected. She was ready to begin a new chapter, with a new job, in a new city.

However, she didn't know that a storm, both literal and financial, was brewing on the horizon.

I met Stella a few months before she became an attending. She had high hopes for her career. After years of sacrificing for her education, she was ready to attack the storm cloud of debt hanging over her head.

In our early conversations, Stella shared her worries. "I owe so much money. How am I ever going to have an actual life? I need to pay off these student loans as soon as possible!" she stressed to me.

I understood her anxiety, but I had a greater concern.

"Stella, I know you are eager to pay down your debt, but there is something much more important we need to focus on first," I advised.

Stella was not afraid to roll up her sleeves and get the work done. Her first job was as a hostess at Red Lobster. She knew her parents could not afford an expensive undergraduate university, so she chose to attend a more modestly priced state school. There, she participated in a work-study program to earn credits, worked two jobs, and became a resident assistant to offset her tuition costs. However, she had known all along that she wanted to attend medical school.

The commitment to medical school required Stella to make tremendous sacrifices. Due to the time and energy needed to be a medical student, she opted for student loans. The promise of a lucrative career as "Dr. Stella" was a compelling reason to say yes to financing her school fees. She graduated four years later with over $300,000 in debt, not including accumulated (and deferred) interest. By the time she completed her four-year residency program, her loans had ballooned to $580,000!

"I feel stuck," she told me during one of our conversations, "It's like an avalanche that is always advancing, and I can't get away from it."

Over the past eight years, every time Stella had received a student loan statement, the balance was noticeably larger than on the previous one. To make matters worse, she had moved for residency without enough money to furnish her apartment, forcing her to use credit cards. When her salary couldn't cover even her basic expenses, credit cards became a bridge and then an anchor.

She came to me after receiving an offer from a hospital in Dallas where she would officially begin working as an attending physician. As we reviewed her contract, Stella insisted, "As soon as I sign this, I'm sending my whole paycheck to my student loans."

I reiterated to her, "We have something far more important we must do first."

"What is that?" she asked with reluctance.

"Build a cash reserve."

"A cash reserve?" She looked at me quizzically. "You mean a rainy-day fund?"

"Yes, that is exactly what I mean," I explained. "After we build this safety net, I am happy to provide you with a plan to get your loans and credit cards paid off as quickly as possible."

Stella took some convincing, but eventually, she decided to trust me. We opened a separate savings account and started funneling 35% of her net paychecks into her reserve.

With a financial cushion in place, Stella took a well-deserved breath. She was finally watching her credit card balance disappear, and her student loan statements were smaller, even if only by a tiny amount each month.

However, she was unhappy in her current role as an attending. She decided a change of scenery was warranted. She applied for a new job in Houston. She was offered the position and subsequently submitted her 90-day notice at the Dallas hospital. Within a few months, she had secured a new apartment and was awaiting her start date. In the gap of time between jobs, she decided to book a dream vacation with her sister to Europe, a celebration of years of sleepless nights, endless shifts, and delayed gratification. After the trip, Stella planned to spend some time with her parents in New York.

While she explored Europe, a storm was brewing back home.

Hurricane Harvey gathered force in the Gulf and struck Houston as a Category 4 storm. By the time Stella boarded her flight back to the US, the storm was impacting the city with life-threatening floods. I recall watching the news as images of her new hospital flashed across the screen. Water rising, patients evacuated, airports closed—it was a disaster.

Stella, still flying over the Atlantic, had no idea what awaited her. I left her a concerned voicemail, "I know you are mid-flight, and you may not have access to any news right now. Your hospital in Houston has been evacuated. I'm glad you'll be with your family in New York, as the airport in your area has been closed. This is out of your control. My advice is that you stay calm, wait for the storm to pass, and formulate a plan."

When she landed, the devastation became clear. She couldn't reach anyone at the hospital. All communication lines were jammed. Her supervisors were unreachable. The news reported that the hospital was underwater and had been closed. What about her apartment? Her car? What about her job?

The answers came a few days later after the storm passed. Her apartment and car were spared. The hospital was not so lucky. The flooding had shut it down indefinitely. Her start date was postponed, postponed again, and then canceled.

Stella faced the worst-case scenario. She had a newly signed lease in a new city with no job and no timeline for when she would be able to return to work. In that moment, she did what a normal person would do—she panicked.

"How am I going to pay my rent? How am I going to pay my bills? I just refinanced my student loan. How will I afford the payments? Where is my money going to come from? What am I going to do?" Stella ranted as she fought back tears of frustration.

"I don't know all of the answers," I replied calmly, "but I am confident you have at least four to five months before you really have to worry about money."

She choked out a laugh. "What the hell are you talking about? How the f*** am I supposed to pay my bills?"

"Easy," I assured her. "With your cash reserve. Remember the rainy-day fund I insisted on before you aggressively paid down your student loans?"

"Wait, how much money do I have in this reserve rainy-day fund?" A hint of optimism crept into her voice.

"Our goal was to build at least a six-month cushion to cover your expenses. You resisted, but we managed to do it. Break glass in case of emergency—your emergency has arrived!"

"Are you telling me I can pay all of my bills for the next three to four months?" she scoffed. "Because that is how long it's going to take me to get credentialed for another job."

"Yes. You're going to be ok. Focus on finding your next role. Don't worry about money right now," I reassured her.

Her savings became her lifeline. It covered rent, food, bills, and a little bit of fun while she searched for another position. Instead of spiraling into debt or desperation, Stella bought herself time and options.

"Every day I wasn't getting paid, I felt the pressure," she later shared with me. "But knowing that I had something to fall back on kept me calm. It gave me space to figure things out."

Ultimately, it took two months to secure a new position at another hospital in Houston. During that time, her cash reserves carried her. Without the rainy-day fund, the floodwaters might have washed away more than her job; they could have drowned her mentally and financially.

Today, Stella is still paying down her student loans. However, she is doing it from a position of strength, not survival. She learned firsthand that while debt reduction is essential, her own financial security is the priority.

Her story isn't one of reckless spending or poor decision-making; it is a reminder that life sometimes brings you storms you cannot predict.

This is why a rainy-day fund is essential. Save your money while the skies are clear so you're ready when the clouds come.

Stella's story demonstrates that savings enable you to adapt to the unexpected. They allow you to adjust your plans, giving you the flexibility to pivot when life's whirlwinds blow you off course.

———————

"You can plan a pretty picnic, but you can't predict the weather."
—Andre 3000, Outkast

REFLECTIVE QUESTIONS

- What would happen to your life if your primary source of income suddenly disappeared for three to six months?
- Are you prioritizing what feels most urgent over what might be most important for your financial security?
- How has your relationship with debt and financial pressure affected your ability to make clear-headed decisions about your future?

———————

DESIGNING LIFE TOGETHER: A STORY OF LOVE, COURAGE, AND FINANCIAL PLANNING

Scott Frank

Stone Steps Financial

THE SAN DIEGO sun shined through my skylight as Brian and Avery settled onto the couch. Avery was full of energy and ready to dive in. Brian was more stoic; it was clear he was a deep thinker from the get-go. The way they chose to sit on the couch spoke of both connection and tension—the kind that comes when two people share a deep love but feel stuck in their lives.

On paper, they embodied success: he, a mechanical engineer at a prestigious medical device company; she, a marketing executive who had carved her path through Fortune 500 consumer goods companies. Yet beneath their professional achievements lay something more compelling: the courage to question whether their current path was the one they truly wanted to walk together.

It was 2019, and at ages 35 and 38, they weren't just seeking financial advice. They were searching for their version of freedom. Like many clients who walk through my door, they thought they were here to discuss money. In reality, they were about to embark on a journey that would transform their lives in ways none of us could have predicted.

As a financial life planner trained in George Kinder's EVOKE process through the Kinder Institute of Life Planning, I've learned that money is simply a tool—albeit a powerful one—for helping people live their best lives. EVOKE (Exploration, Vision, Obstacles, Knowledge, and Execution) provides a framework for diving deeper than traditional financial planning, helping clients discover and achieve what truly matters to them.

During our initial Exploration phase, Brian and Avery each had individual conversations with me about what constituted a great life. While one spoke, I asked the other to listen and let them know I would check in with them to hear what they felt was most important to their partner. Like most clients, they started with financial topics—homeownership in San Diego's challenging market, retirement savings, investment strategies. Once they knew we could handle those issues and asked, "Anything else?" the real story began to unfold.

Brian, despite his success in medical device engineering, harbored a passion for sustainability that he couldn't ignore. He longed to make a meaningful impact on environmental issues, to be more present in his relationship with Avery, to deepen connections with his family, and to leave a lasting mark on the world. His eyes lit up when he spoke about sustainable innovation, but dimmed when describing his current role. He felt stuck and was unsure about how to proceed, held back not just by practical considerations but also by a deep-rooted scarcity mindset that made big changes feel risky.

Avery had already taken a bold step, leaving her corporate career to build a wellness company focused on yoga and life coaching. But her dreams extended beyond entrepreneurship. She yearned to become a mother, to help teenagers find their path, to explore the world, and to heal a strained relationship with her own mother. Time was a constant presence in her mind—both the ticking of her biological clock and the sense that life was passing too quickly in the pursuit of conventional success.

The beauty of the EVOKE process lies in its ability to create space for couples to understand their own desires and their partner's dreams as well. Through guided questions and deep listening, Brian and Avery began to see how they could support each other's aspirations, even when their immediate goals differed.

As we moved into the Vision phase, we took time to chat deeply about their answers to inspirations exercises and then painted a detailed picture of their ideal future for each of them. You see, couples are not one cohort, but rather two individuals who chose to walk through life together. The process revealed that their seemingly different paths shared common threads: a desire for meaningful work, the freedom to make bold choices, and the ability to impact others positively.

In the Obstacles phase, we repainted their visions and asked: What could possibly get in the way? We then worked through each point systematically. San Diego's housing market seemed an insurmountable barrier to homeownership. Career transitions felt risky. Starting a family amidst so much change appeared daunting. For each challenge, we explored what they could do, how they could do it, when they could do it, and who would hold them accountable. While we didn't solve all their differences about starting a family in our meetings together, they were committed to finding a solution that honored both their individual journeys and their shared dreams.

Through the Knowledge and Execution phases, we developed concrete strategies to align their resources—not just money, but also time, energy, and talent—with their vision. I reminded them that these four resources are interchangeable, and sometimes investing in one can yield returns in another.

What happened next demonstrates the transformative power of financial life planning. Brian and Avery made the bold decision to leave San Diego, returning to Avery's hometown where housing was more affordable. This move solved their housing challenge and opened up possibilities they hadn't imagined. They purchased not one but two homes, creating both stability and opportunity.

With the foundation of a solid financial plan supporting them, they each pursued their passions with renewed vigor. Brian enrolled in a master's program in sustainability, launching entrepreneurial ventures that aligned with his values. His journey led him to a role he hadn't dreamed possible—heading up packaging sustainability for a Fortune 500 company, where he could make an impact at scale.

Avery's path took unexpected turns as well. Her experience in wellness and corporate marketing merged beautifully when she returned to the corporate world. She began leading sustainability initiatives and successfully guided her division to B Corp certification—a rigorous standard that proves a company is using business as a force for good in the world. She discovered she could create even greater positive change by bringing her wellness-centered mindset into the corporate world. Her role now allows her to influence how a major company impacts both people and planet, touching far more lives than she could have imagined when she first dreamed of helping others.

Their journey to parenthood ultimately led them to IVF, a path that tested their emotional and financial resilience. Brian later reflected on this challenging period: "While Avery shouldered the immediate physical burden, I felt the weight of our future shared finances. Your financial guidance based on our work with the EVOKE process gave us the confidence to proceed without the added stress of questioning whether it was what both of us really wanted and if we could afford it. This honestly prevented many heated arguments during an already challenging time."

When they finally welcomed their daughter into the world, she became the love of their lives. Brian loves biking her to daycare before he bikes to work, even in the rain; he doesn't just work in sustainability now, he lives it!

Their story illustrates that financial planning, when done right, is about more than money. It's about creating the space and security to pursue what matters most. It's about understanding that true wealth isn't measured solely in dollars but in the ability to live authentically and purposefully.

Today, Avery and Brian continue to evolve and grow. Their journey reminds us that financial planning isn't just about securing a comfortable retirement or maximizing investment returns. It's about creating a life of meaning, purpose, and possibility—a life where money serves as a tool for flourishing rather than a measure of success.

As I watch them navigate their new life—Brian making waves in sustainable packaging, Avery leading corporate responsibility initiatives, both of them embracing parenthood and homeownership—I'm reminded why I chose this profession. Real financial planning is about helping people write their own stories of transformation, one chapter at a time.

Looking at Brian and Avery's story through a wider lens, their journey reflects timeless wisdom about the nature of true contentment. When they first arrived in my office, they embodied a paradox familiar to many successful professionals—the more they achieved, the more elusive satisfaction became. Their corporate achievements and material success hadn't brought the peace they sought.

The EVOKE process helped them develop a deeper awareness of their authentic selves. Through our conversations, Brian began to process and understand his deep-rooted scarcity mindset—a fear that had kept him tethered to his secure but unfulfilling career. By exploring his true aspirations and examining his relationship with financial security, he found the clarity and peace of mind to fully commit to their shared journey. This internal transformation was crucial to every change that followed—from their move to a new city to his career shift into sustainability.

Their transformation illustrates the profound power of aligning work with values. Brian didn't just switch jobs; he chose a path of positive impact through sustainability. Avery's journey from corporate marketing to wellness teaching and back to corporate responsibility shows that meaningful work isn't about a specific job, but about how it serves others while bringing personal fulfillment.

Their story also demonstrates the interconnected nature of all things. Their individual dreams, initially seeming in conflict, were actually complementary. Brian's desire for sustainability work and Avery's calling to help others merged into harmonious paths. Their move away from San Diego's expensive housing market enabled both their professional transformations and their dream of parenthood.

Perhaps most powerfully, they learned to hold their goals lightly. While they had clear intentions—homeownership, career changes, starting a family—they remained open to how these might unfold. This openness to possibility, rather than rigid attachment to specific outcomes, paradoxically helped them achieve even more than they'd initially imagined.

Most profound was their evolving understanding of wealth itself. They came to see that true abundance isn't about accumulating more but about having enough to live authentically. Their story reminds us that financial planning, at its best, isn't about maximizing wealth but about funding a life of meaning.

After all, the best stories never really end—they keep unfolding in new and unexpected ways, teaching us that life's greatest wealth comes not from what we have, but from who we become.

———————

As you read Brian and Avery's story, you might wonder how to begin your own journey of discovery. The EVOKE process, developed by George Kinder and the Kinder Institute of Life Planning, offers powerful tools to help you uncover what matters most. While working with a trained financial life planner provides the most comprehensive experience, you can begin your exploration with the fundamental tool that helped Brian and Avery: The Three Questions.

REFLECTIVE QUESTIONS

The Three Questions, which must be considered in sequence, invite increasingly deeper reflection about what truly matters in your life:

1. Imagine you are financially secure, that you have enough money to take care of your needs, now and in the future. How would you live your life? Would you change anything? Let yourself go. Don't hold back on your dreams. Describe a life that is complete and richly yours.
2. This time you visit your doctor, who tells you that you have only five to ten years to live. The good news is you won't ever feel sick. The bad news is you will have no notice of the moment of your death. What will you do in the time you have remaining? Will you change your life and how will you do it?
3. This time your doctor shocks you with the news that you only have one day left to live. Notice what feelings arise as you confront your very real mortality. Ask yourself:

    *   What did I miss?
    *   Who did I not get to be?
    *   What did I not get to do?

The Three Questions were developed by George Kinder and the Kinder Institute of Life Planning. These questions are powerful and are best used with trained guidance.

SUMMARY OF MONEY IS FOR...
Changing

CHANGE IS THE great disruptor. And the great revealer.

Life doesn't always ask permission before it shifts. A partner is lost. A dream evolves. A storm arrives. And in those moments, money becomes more than a plan; it becomes a partner in resilience.

In these stories, change wasn't just survived, it was honored. Legacies were reimagined. New definitions of success were formed.

Each story reminds us: money can't stop change, but it can support transformation. It can buy us time. It can offer new choices. It can help us move forward, even when we're afraid.

Because change doesn't mean losing control.

Sometimes, it's the beginning of finally claiming it.

DESIGN YOUR FINANCIAL LIFE: MONEY IS FOR...
Changing

Get clear on the numbers

Income

- [ ] What is your total household income?
- [ ] How stable is this income? (W-2, 1099, business ownership, multiple income streams)
- [ ] What are your income growth prospects over the next three to five years?
- [ ] Do you have any irregular income sources? (bonuses, freelance work, rental income, gifts)

Where does your income go?

- [ ] Taxes: Federal, state, local, FICA, property taxes
- [ ] Fixed obligations: Mortgage/rent, insurance premiums, minimum debt payments, utilities
- [ ] Debt payments: Credit cards, student loans, car loans, personal loans
- [ ] What are the interest rates and minimum payments?
- [ ] Savings: Emergency fund, short-term goals

☐ Investing: 401(k), IRA, taxable accounts, other investments

☐ Spending: Groceries, transportation, entertainment, subscriptions, miscellaneous

Changing preparedness

☐ Of those expenses, what are truly non-negotiable even in a crisis?

☐ How long will your current cash reserves last if income stops completely?

☐ What's your target emergency fund size? (three to six months of essential expenses is common)

☐ Do you have a systematic plan to build your emergency fund?

☐ Are there other financial safety nets? (spouse's income, family support, insurance policies)

Get help

☐ What specific expertise gaps do you have? (tax planning, investment strategy, estate planning)

☐ Is there a trusted advisor, family member, or guide who can help you.

☐ Do you have accountability partners for your financial goals?

☐ Are there financial communities or groups you could join for ongoing support and learning?

MONEY IS FOR...
Dreaming

MODERN SOCIETY OFTEN values money as a measure of professional and personal success, but it should also be viewed as a means to bring our deepest dreams to life.

For many, dreams and dollars live in separate worlds. We grow up learning how to save, how to invest, and how to plan. Yet rarely are we taught how to use money as a tool to imagine, to hope, or to build something meaningful that wasn't there before. That's what this section is about: reclaiming the right to dream and allowing money to support the vision rather than define its limits.

These stories are not about windfalls or overnight achievements. They're about real people using intentional choices, courage, creativity, and sometimes unconventional planning to pursue what matters most—from starting a family to building a cabin in the forest, walking to the ocean they've always loved, or leaving a stable job to follow a deeper calling.

What unites them is the belief that dreams are worth fighting for, and that financial planning isn't just about preparing for the future—it's about making space for life right now.

Because money, when aligned with purpose, becomes more than spreadsheets and savings goals.

It becomes a bridge between the life you have… and the life you long for.

ALIGNING DREAMS
AND DOLLARS

Justin Castelli, RLP®, CFP®
Santiago

"**I** CAN'T DO THIS anymore."

I knew it was coming, but it still came as a shock the day Kendrick spoke those words.

"I dread going to work. It doesn't fulfill me. I'm not really making an impact on the world. And, if I'm being honest, my views and values don't align with the institution of healthcare. The worst part of all of this is that the unhappiness from my work is beginning to impact how I show up as a husband and a father, and I can't have that.

"I just can't do this anymore."

IT ALWAYS STARTS WITH A TRADITIONAL APPROACH TO FINANCIAL PLANNING

I've known Kendrick and Whitney for years; we knew each other earlier in our lives and reconnected when I launched my firm in 2015. The timing was perfect; they were looking for a financial advisor, and my new firm was actively seeking to work with young professionals. At the time, Kendrick was working in hospital administration—quickly advancing up the corporate ladder in pursuit of his goal to become the CEO of a hospital system—Whitney was an elementary school teacher, and they had just welcomed their first child into the world.

Our relationship began as most financial planning relationships do: planning for retirement, college, and, for Kendrick and Whitney, a second home somewhere warm in the future—most likely Florida. In addition to the traditional goals, we also addressed the needs for life insurance, supplementary disability insurance, and proper estate planning documents. We made sure their long-term plan supported their desire to experience life along the way; Kendrick and Whitney did not want to miss the opportunity to travel, create memories, and experience life as they prepared for their ambitious long-term goals.

Our plan ensured:

- 401(k)s and 403(b)s were maxed out.
- Health Savings Accounts (HSAs) were maxed out.
- Roth IRAs were established.
- A taxable investment account was started to provide flexibility with access to assets along the way.

Kendrick and Whitney aggressively funded these accounts with the expectation that they would be needed to help them reach early retirement goals, have that second house, and make sure their kids could have a college experience and every opportunity to get off to a good start in their adult lives.

Their financial plan was strong and off to a great start.

LIFE BRINGS OPPORTUNITIES

Over the years I spent working with them, their family grew with one more child, Kendrick continued to ascend toward the CEO position, and Whitney stepped away from teaching to spend more time with the kids. Eventually, Kendrick was offered a new opportunity in another state that would move him one step closer to achieving his goal of becoming CEO.

This presented the first opportunity for Kendrick and Whitney to do something untraditional, at least in terms of financial planning.

On their first visit to their soon-to-be new state, Kendrick and Whitney fell in love with a house they just knew would be the perfect home to start the next chapter of their lives. The only problem was they had not even put their home on the market yet. When they made their trip, they had no expectations of finding, let alone making an offer on, a home. But something about the house felt right to them, and after a couple of phone calls, we devised a plan that probably wouldn't be found in a financial planning textbook.

Since Kendrick had already accepted the new position, we worked quickly to find a solution that would allow them to purchase the home. Our strategy to fund their down payment was to roll over his old 401(k) to the new hospital's 401(k) plan and then take a loan. We had explored other options, including taking a home equity loan, but this would have taken too long and been difficult to secure due to the recent employment change. Therefore, after discussing the pros and cons of taking a 401(k) loan and developing an accelerated repayment plan for once their home was sold, Kendrick and Whitney ultimately decided this loan was the best strategy for them.

They were able to secure their dream home in their new state.

WITH MORE LIFE EXPERIENCE, GOALS TEND TO EVOLVE

As Kendrick, Whitney, and the kids established themselves in their new community, Kendrick continued to be a high performer at work, which brought him into contact with new people and exposure to another side of healthcare—the technology space, or healthtech. This introduction would eventually wake an entrepreneur in Kendrick he didn't know existed and become the catalyst for a pursuit of more purpose and impact.

In our review meetings, Kendrick's vision and goals began to drift from the traditional goals he and Whitney had originally set. Retirement, college, and the vacation home were still important, but not the priority they once were. Their goals were shifting to align with who they had become over the years and with their evolving values. Kendrick began expressing frustration with the healthcare system's focus on treatment over prevention and the slow pace of change. He started questioning the goal he once thought he was destined to achieve—CEO.

Instead of strategizing his next move to rise higher, Kendrick talked more about the excitement he saw in the healthtech space. He met and befriended people in the industry who began to take notice of him.

It was obvious his passion had shifted from healthcare administration to healthtech.

I got into healthcare following my why, my purpose, and upon getting there, climbing the mountain and seeing what was in front of me after going so far, so quickly in my career, I realized that my goals and dreams of truly changing the industry were not going to be attainable from the inside out. So, I had to deal with the process of grieving the achievement of a dream that was not going to end the way I wanted it to and pivot to a new future, following that pursuit, if you will.

—Kendrick

FOLLOWING YOUR DREAMS MAY REQUIRE CHANGE

A few years passed, and Kendrick's frustration with his inability to make a greater impact continued to grow, culminating in the moment that opened this chapter. Discontent at work was beginning to impact Kendrick's personal life, and that was the final straw. Initially, he didn't know exactly how, but he wanted to explore possibilities outside the safe and comfortable world of healthcare.

Unlike many who complain without action, Kendrick sought ways to move forward.

We discussed how he could build his personal brand to be known as a visionary and leader in healthcare, beyond his current circle. He identified healthtech companies he was connected with and explored offering his consulting services. He worked through the non-financial aspects of a potential career transition and ensured Whitney was fully on board.

With a clear vision, positive feedback, and Whitney's support, it was time to revisit their financial plan and update it for the new life Kendrick was designing; it was time to shift their financial plan from the life they thought they were supposed to live to the life they knew they now wanted to live.

THE VISION

Kendrick had a unique perspective once he discovered his new path.

He could see how technology could solve many of healthcare's problems—something many of his corporate peers either couldn't see or refused to acknowledge. Alongside his vision, he had 20 years of experience and deep industry contacts. Kendrick could become the bridge between the healthtech world and the traditional healthcare system.

With this vision in mind, he designed a plan to launch his consulting business, determined the financial metrics required for him to leave his corporate role, and addressed the key benefits he would be losing—health insurance, disability coverage, and retirement matches.

Looking back, little did we know that when we first started their financial plan, we were not just planning for retirement—we were building the freedom to pursue dreams yet to be discovered.

MAKING THE DREAM A REALITY

Less than a year after moving from "it would be nice if…" to "let's see if we can make this work," Kendrick secured the consulting engagements he needed to replace their required take-home income. After receiving one final bonus, he left the hospital system and launched his consulting business.

Today, Kendrick is no longer just chasing titles—he's living a life of impact, fulfillment, and alignment. His story is a reminder that money isn't just for retirement or rainy days—it's for dreaming, evolving, and creating a life that feels true. When you align your financial plan with who you are and who you're becoming, you give yourself permission to dream bigger—and the means to make those dreams real.

REFLECTIVE QUESTIONS

- Are you building wealth strategically to achieve your dream future, or are you just following the traditional financial planning playbook?
- How much financial flexibility have you built into your life to pursue unexpected opportunities or make major changes?
- What would you do differently with your career and life if money weren't the primary constraint?

NAVIGATING THE BABY PRICE TAG

Jessica Davis, CFP®
Peterson Row Advisory

"They couldn't afford to have a baby—until they practiced having one first. With every dollar they set aside, the impossible slowly transformed into inevitable."

L ESLIE DEEPLY WANTED to become a mother. In their Dublin home—the area they had chosen specifically for its community and proximity to their support network of friends—Leslie and Kyle had established their life together. Though they jokingly called their neighborhood "poor Dublin" compared to the wealthier parts of town, they valued the community and saw it as an ideal place to raise a family.

BABY DREAMS VERSUS BUDGET REALITY

While Leslie felt the pull of motherhood with every fiber of her being, Kyle saw the reality of their finances standing in their way. It wasn't that Kyle didn't want children. It was that he was the pragmatic, financially cautious spouse who couldn't see a path forward.

"Leslie wanted a baby right away, but I kept looking at our budget and seeing red flags," Kyle explains. "With her student loans already taking $1,000 a month and daycare potentially adding another $1,500, the math just didn't work in our minds."

Their approaches to money reflected their different backgrounds. Kyle's mother worked as a Chief Financial Officer, giving him early exposure to financial planning. Leslie came from a hardworking family where her father drove trucks and her mother worked as a secretary, but financial literacy wasn't part of her upbringing. "When I needed student loans for college," Leslie explains, "I didn't have much guidance. My dad would say, 'Go ask your brother what to do,' and my brother, not knowing much more himself, would say, 'Just take out the maximum.'"

While Leslie's family was hardworking and provided all they could, they did not have access to formal financial education and primarily understood college as an investment in the future. At the time, they weren't fully aware of how student loans could compound over time.

This gap in financial knowledge had created an unspoken tension in their relationship when it came to having children. Leslie's timeline for starting a family—roughly a year after their 2018 wedding—kept colliding with Kyle's more cautious outlook.

"I had every ounce of my body wanting to have a baby," Leslie says. "But Kyle was resistant because of the financials. I started questioning myself: we have good jobs and a house in a decent neighborhood. Can we really not afford to have a child?"

As a financial advisor, when I first heard Leslie express this tension during our meetings, I recognized a pattern I've seen with many couples: deeply personal dreams colliding with financial realities. My role wasn't to judge who was right, but to find a path forward they could both embrace.

BREAKING THE SILENCE AND FINDING FINANCIAL GUIDANCE

It was Kyle's mother who suggested they meet with a financial advisor and introduced them to her own firm. That connection led them to me, a financial advisor of a similar age who immediately understood their situation.

"I thought financial advisors were only for rich people," Leslie says. "I didn't realize they could help people like us who were just trying to figure out how to make things happen."

When Leslie and Kyle first came to my office, I could see there was more than just numbers at stake. During one of our early meetings, Leslie's eyes filled with tears when she talked about wanting to start a family.

I approached their situation holistically because it was about much more than debt ratios, savings, or income. We needed to find a path forward that would flip their negative net worth into positive territory while also honoring their priorities. The challenge wasn't just mathematical—it was emotional.

REHEARSING FOR PARENTHOOD

Together, we created a strategy to see if we could make the financially 'impossible,' possible. This began with Kyle and Leslie researching the actual costs of having a baby and setting aside that amount each month to 'practice' for this reality.

This 'baby fund' would serve two purposes: testing whether they could handle the financial strain of childcare costs while simultaneously building a financial cushion for when they actually had a child. The approach was essentially a financial simulation, allowing them to experience the impact before making the actual commitment.

The approach immediately resonated. "It 100% brought down my anxiety," Leslie says. "There was so much less stress just seeing what was actually possible. We get stuck in our minds, building up these stories that we can't do things. This showed me it was possible."

I also encouraged them to start asking friends and neighbors about childcare options beyond expensive daycare centers. Not all options cost $1,500 a month, and in a family-friendly community like Dublin, creative solutions often exist if you know where to look.

Through their network of friends, they discovered Mary, an experienced caregiver who charged much less than a corporate daycare. "This woman has been doing this for 30 years. She is an angel on earth," Leslie shares.

But the most surprising childcare solution came from family. Kyle's parents decided to relocate from Dayton to Columbus, with his father, Alan, offering to care for their future child two days a week.

While they practiced setting aside money for future childcare, they also took practical steps to prepare financially. Leslie picked up extra speech pathology work on weekends to save for a new SUV, which she ultimately purchased with cash. "I wanted an SUV for when our baby arrived, and not having a car payment made our monthly expenses more manageable."

Leslie also began educating herself about personal finance, listening to podcasts, and asking questions during their meetings with me. "I was determined to learn as much about our money as I could," she explains. "I wanted to understand what we were doing and why."

Kyle became a weekend wedding photographer, methodically adding to their savings while learning financial flexibility. His parents had instilled careful planning habits in him, but the practice method helped him see that rigid timelines weren't always necessary.

What I admired about Leslie and Kyle was their willingness to play the hand they were dealt. Instead of waiting for the perfect financial circumstances, they found creative ways to make progress with their current reality.

CREATING FINANCIAL TRANSFORMATION THROUGH INTENTIONAL CHOICES

Month by month, as their "baby fund" grew, so did their confidence. They also took additional financial steps—refinancing their mortgage to take advantage of lower interest rates and adding those savings to their nest egg. These small financial decisions created momentum in their journey.

"After being introduced to Mary and experiencing those monthly payments coming out, we started to feel stable," Leslie recalls. "By early 2020, even with the pandemic starting and us both working with Covid patients in the hospital, we felt ready."

November 2020 brought life-changing news: Leslie was pregnant.

"I personally felt prepared," she says. "Of course, there's anxiety around parenthood, but financially, we had already created a roadmap and demonstrated it was possible. We wanted to make sure that if we were going to bring a child into this life, we could provide something financially stable for them."

Their daughter Rae arrived the following summer, entering a family that had transformed its financial situation through intentional choices and careful planning. With Rae's arrival came new financial considerations. They set up life insurance policies to protect their growing family, discussed guardianship plans, and even started a college fund for her—financial steps that would have seemed overwhelming just two years earlier.

Fast forward two more years, and they had built a positive net worth in the six figures. That's an incredible turnaround from where they started. This transformation wasn't about sudden windfalls or dramatic income changes—it came from consistent application of sound financial principles.

Both Leslie and Kyle eventually found new, better-paying positions, increasing their household income. But the foundation for their success had been built before those opportunities materialized—

through the financial habits and mindset shifts they'd developed along the way.

LIVING THEIR DREAM WITH PURPOSE

Today, Leslie and Kyle continue using the "practice" method for new expenses. As Rae approaches preschool age, they're already setting aside money to adjust to those costs, creating a financial buffer before the actual expense arrives.

"We're doing that nesting thing again," Leslie explains from their living room, now dotted with colorful toys and children's books. "The financial costs are going to increase for preschool, so we're putting that away and practicing now. It's become second nature to us."

Their approach to money has fundamentally changed. "It feels more controlled," Leslie says. "Financial planning isn't just for rich people—it's about feeling secure and stable."

This newfound financial confidence has led to thoughtful decisions about their family's future. "We know that given our situation, we probably couldn't bring another child into this world and provide the same lifestyle. That's good insight for us—not a limitation but a conscious choice about how we want to shape our family's future."

Perhaps the most beautiful outcome of their journey has been watching the relationship between Rae and her "Papa" Alan flourish. "My father-in-law is the most loving, attentive, and joyful Papa you could imagine," Leslie shares. "He happily embraces Rae's glitter and tutus while also introducing her to his favorite music, like Pink Floyd. They've developed the most beautiful bond."

This creative childcare arrangement, combining Mary's affordable care with Alan's grandparent care, has provided Rae with loving attention while keeping costs manageable. The arrangement also saves them significant costs per month compared to traditional daycare centers, allowing them to allocate those funds to other priorities like Rae's college fund. It's a perfect example of how thinking beyond conventional solutions can yield benefits far greater than just financial savings.

Leslie is also determined to give Rae a strong financial foundation from the start. "I want to teach her about savings accounts and watching her money grow. I didn't know anything about the stock market until my 30s, so I'd love to teach her how it works and maybe even put in a little for her that she can watch grow over the years."

As their advisor, watching their transformation has been deeply rewarding. I've seen many clients struggle with the financial implications of parenthood, but Leslie and Kyle show that with planning and practice, even the most daunting financial barriers can become stepping stones. Their journey wasn't about having perfect finances before starting a family—it was about creating a practical path forward and then following it with discipline and creativity.

Leslie now advocates for others to seek financial guidance without letting ego get in the way. "Put your arrogance aside and collaborate with somebody to really progress yourself," she advises. "There's going to be insights and experiences that you have no idea about, and finding a trusted person you can go to is probably the most beneficial thing you could do."

From a negative net worth and seemingly impossible dreams to a thriving family with a secure financial foundation, Leslie and Kyle's story demonstrates that money truly is for dreaming—but those dreams require both practical planning and the courage to take the first step, even when the path isn't completely clear.

What once seemed impossible—having a baby despite daunting financial barriers—has become reality through practice, planning, and the courage to take that first step into the unknown.

REFLECTIVE QUESTIONS

- What dream feels financially out of reach in your life right now?
- How might "practicing" the financial impact of your dream change your perspective?
- What creative solutions or family resources might you be overlooking?
- How can you use your current financial reality as a starting point rather than waiting for ideal circumstances?

FROM DIRT TO DREAM: HOW A DARING VISION BECAME A HOME, A LEGACY, AND A LIFE

Nick Covyeau, CFP®
Swell Financial

WHAT HAPPENS WHEN the dream of rugged freedom in the wilderness collides with decades of financial caution?

Rocky and Lu's story is one of sacrifice, generosity, and the pursuit of dreams.

It all began with a simple family road trip. Twenty-five years ago, Rocky and Lu packed their bags, loaded up the car, and left their crowded Southern California home behind, heading north as the mountains called to them. They wove their way through some of the best National Parks of the Pacific Northwest—through ancient forests, alongside crystal lakes, and beneath towering peaks. The beauty of the wilderness stood in stark contrast to their busy suburban lives.

Somewhere between the winding forest roads and open mountain skies, a vision was born. The couple fell in love with the wild beauty of the region and began to dream of one day owning their own piece of it.

That dream took shape slowly but deliberately. For eight years they searched, hoping for a plot of land that would speak to them. A little bit like Goldilocks, if you will, scouring internet listings of small acreage properties.

Over time, the dream became clearer and clearer—one stream of water, no, two streams. Now let's make it border a National Forest…

SAYING "YES" TO THE DREAM

At some point, reality sets in and those dreams are tested. Is buying this plot of land really a good financial decision?

Rocky and Lu had very modest careers but managed to put their two kids through college. Rocky worked hard in the manufacturing industry to provide for his family. Lu began substitute teaching once the kids were old enough and later became the school librarian.

They believed in the value of education, working hard, saving diligently, and staying out of debt. They did whatever it took to get through each month, eventually sending their two incredible children through graduate school and helping them out financially wherever they could.

Still, budgeting was a necessity and money was never in excess. Around every corner was always the question:

"Can we afford this? Do we have enough?"

So how was a giant plot of land, more than a thousand miles away and without a home built on it yet, supposed to fit into their lives?

Having stayed true to their values over all these years—living beneath their means to keep a dream alive—they had positioned themselves, now in their 50s, to make a real go at this.

Financial Planner Nick here. Though I wasn't yet part of Rocky and Lu's story, if I had been at the time, I would have had significant questions about this major financial decision: Just because you can technically afford a retirement dream property doesn't mean it's automatically a great financial idea.

One of my favorite exercises to go through with clients is helping them align their money with their time, energy, and passions, and identify the barriers standing in their way.

Had we met, what we would have most likely arrived at was that this dream was too tight financially today but not impossible if it's truly what they most wanted.

Yes, they were debt-free at the time, having worked tirelessly to pay off their home. But were they really ready to take on an even bigger mortgage this close to retirement?

"Growing up without much, and now we're mortgaging our home to buy dirt?" Lu remembered thinking.

"You're crazy," their friends told them.

And to be honest, deep down, they knew it too.

Oftentimes, Rocky would ask himself, "Are we making a huge mistake? Will we end up regretting this? It feels like going against every sound financial decision we've ever made."

They had worked so hard to pay off their mortgage, putting their kids through college... were they really going to do this?

FAITH AND TRUST BECAME THEIR GUIDE

The tension was real. But even more real was their conviction and commitment to the dream. It was unshakable.

Rocky, the ever-steady partner, looked at Lu and simply said, "As long as we're happy, we'll find a way to make this work."

Faith became their guide over the next eight years. Rocky and Lu held their dream loosely, allowing their faith to orchestrate the timing and find their dream plot of land while they patiently and prayerfully waited. They believed if it was meant to be, then the rest would figure itself out.

And then it happened.

That "just right" property finally appeared in their inbox.

117.5 beautiful acres completely surrounded by National Forest, with creeks winding through and butterflies dancing in a meadow of wildflowers—they knew they'd finally found their home.

But when the property came on the market, new challenges appeared.

How were they going to qualify for a mortgage on such a large property? Could they get financing in place before another offer appeared?

"Our realtor told us, 'It's yours if you can get us the funds within 30 days. Otherwise, it's gone,'" Lu recalled.

Rocky and Lu prayed fervently, asking, "If this is right, let it be."

The timing was so tight that they called the bank nearly every day, praying that the financing would come through.

And then they waited…

And waited.

And waited.

With less than three hours left on the realtor's deadline and still no word yet, they felt as if all hope had been lost and that surely the owners had accepted another offer.

But then the phone rang.

The financing had come through and their offer was accepted.

117.5 acres of butterflies, elk, and wildflowers were theirs.

They were meant to be stewards of that land. Yes, land. Not a house. Just raw, undeveloped land.

They got what they had wanted, and now, it was time to get to work.

KEEPING THE WILDERNESS DREAM ALIVE FOR 20+ YEARS

Rocky and Lu's dreamy property didn't materialize overnight.

What many now see today as a charming little cabin nestled deep in a National Forest took nearly 25 years of holding onto a dream and a vision.

The vision was born on that legendary road trip in 2000. The perfect plot of land appeared ten years later.

It took them ten more years of backbreaking labor to finish building their home. For the first four years, Rocky and Lu spent every summer vacation clearing out the property and constructing the road they needed to build their future house.

While still working full-time before retirement, Rocky and Lu used every single one of their allotted vacation days to make the grueling drive between Southern California and the Pacific Northwest, to clear the homesite, and build the bones of the home by hand.

Most trips, Rocky and Lu camped in the bed of their truck with their dog, using a five-gallon basin and a shower head as their only source of bathing.

These trips weren't glamorous, but building their home themselves felt sacred. Every trip, every nail, every ache was a step closer to the dream they both saw so clearly.

REALIZING THE DREAM MEANT LETTING GO OF THE PAST

In 2017, our paths crossed at a pivotal moment. I met Rocky and Lu while they were caring for Lu's mother, Dottie, in the family home where Lu had grown up—a place filled with decades of memories. They faced the emotional weight of a critical financial decision.

Years earlier, Lu's father had made her promise never to sell the family home. To him, that modest house represented their family's approach to life—living simply, saving carefully, and giving generously whenever they could. Their home wasn't fancy, but it was paid for, and it stood as a reminder that you didn't need much to live well and help others along the way.

Now she stood at a crossroads: honor that promise or pursue the dream she and Rocky had nurtured for nearly two decades. They needed to sell Dottie's house to pay off the remaining mortgage on their Pacific Northwest land and fund the completion of the dream cabin.

What changed everything was a memorable trip they took with Dottie.

Standing among the trees with butterflies dancing through wildflowers, Dottie turned to her daughter and said words Lu would never forget: "Let's sell the house and move up here." With those simple words, she gave Lu profound permission to go against her father's wishes.

"Mom had seen how happy this place made us," Lu later told me. "She knew it was where our hearts belonged. It was the blessing I needed to let go."

That's the beautiful reality of life—as one chapter closes, another begins. As we sat together planning, I realized Rocky and Lu already had the answers within themselves; they just needed permission to move forward with their journey.

After Dottie passed away, their emotions were raw, their questions fundamental: "What do we do now?" As their financial advisor, I saw my role not as a numbers-cruncher but as a guide through this transition.

Rocky and Lu needed to make some critical financial decisions while navigating their grief. They had to list and sell the house, hire contractors to get it ready, and finally unpack all of Dottie's finances and different policies. Together, we worked tirelessly to check each item off the list one by one.

The proceeds from selling Dottie's house would be the key to realizing their dream—paying off their land, covering the final construction expenses, and funding their retirement.

And as difficult a decision as it ultimately was to sell the family house, Rocky and Lu realized that as they let go of one family dream, a new one was being born.

My role wasn't to make decisions for them but to create clarity in a fog of emotion. "We trust you," they said simply, placing the substantial proceeds from the sale in my hands. For Rocky and Lu, this wasn't just money; it was the fruit of multiple generations of stewardship and the seed of their own legacy.

Financial planning, at its heart, isn't about spreadsheets and numbers. It's about helping people transform their values into financial reality. My job was to organize the pieces so their two-decade dream could finally materialize, turning the ending of one cherished family home into the beginning of another.

In late 2023, over 20 years after their original road trip, they walked hand in hand through the front door of their completed cabin.

CREATING A NEW FAMILY LEGACY— WITH NO STRINGS ATTACHED

Today, Rocky and Lu see money differently. It's no longer about scraping by or working multiple jobs to survive. It's about presence— being with family, giving generously, and preparing a legacy not just in dollars, but also in dreams.

Time is their new currency.

Every day when they wake up in their mountain home, they see their faith reflected back to them. They see God's fingerprints in how everything fell into place, how each challenge was overcome, how their dream materialized despite the odds.

Their land has grown in value, yes, but that's not important to them as much as they cherish their role to be stewards of that special land—to care for it, protect it, and conserve it.

They've established their land as a sanctuary, prohibiting hunting and trapping to protect the forest for generations to come.

Legacy, to them, isn't about forcing the next generation to love the land the way they do. It's about giving their kids and grandkids the freedom to dream their own dreams. When asked about their legacy and what it means to them, Lu said: "A legacy is something that *you* enjoy and something you only *hope* your kids will enjoy. Our children may never want to live here, and that's okay."

When I visited Rocky and Lu in 2022, I stood beside them on their balcony overlooking the mountains they now called home. "Sometimes I can't believe we actually did it," Lu marveled.

What struck me most wasn't just the beauty of their property, but how this shared dream had deepened their relationship. After 45 years of marriage and countless challenges overcome together, their partnership had only grown stronger through each obstacle, each loan rejection, each backbreaking weekend of construction, each moment of doubt.

"Money worried us for so many years," Rocky reflected. "Now we see it differently. It wasn't about having more—it was about using what we had to build something meaningful."

That's the wisdom many of us miss. We often see only someone's finish line, their dream fulfilled, without seeing the thousands of small sacrifices and acts of faith that made it possible. For Rocky and Lu, transforming money from a source of anxiety into a tool for creating meaning is perhaps their greatest achievement.

REFLECTIVE QUESTIONS

- What is your dream?
- What would you do if money weren't an obstacle?
- How committed would you be to see that dream become a reality?
- What dream or value is driving every money decision in your life?

CATCHING THE WAVE
OF A LIFETIME

Tyler Aubrey, CFP®
Define Financial

Tom and stacy came from modest roots—the kind that teaches you to stretch a dollar, fix what's broken, and never say yes to an extra luxury without sleeping on it for a few nights first. They had mastered the art of saving, maxing out their retirement accounts, avoiding unnecessary debt, and earning healthy pensions, but they had never quite practiced the art of spending.

Tom knew the ocean better than anyone. As an oceanographer, surfer, and former lifeguard, he could read the rhythm of the waves and predict the sets with magnificent accuracy. He had surfed all over the Pacific—from home in Southern California to the less-traveled, rugged shores of Central America, and idyllic islands of the South Pacific. But for him, home had always been this stretch of Southern California coastline. Short of a daily offshore breeze and a long-period swell, Tom had nearly everything he needed to build a happy life.

Stacy, on the other hand, was a recently retired pharmacist who now found her rhythm in more quiet routines—morning walks with their dog, swimming, hiking nearby trails, and pursuing her passions of photography, gardening, and painting. Her artistry was less about bold color and more about soft, purposeful imagery. And the beach showed up often in her work, not just as a backdrop, but also as a character—shifting and evolving, much like the life she and Tom had built together.

For 30 years, Tom and Stacy lived just over a mile from the ocean—not on the beachfront, but close enough to hear the waves on a quiet night and catch the colorful sunsets pouring in through their family room window most afternoons.

Like the persistent waves washing away footprints on the beach, many things had come and gone in those 30 years. Their starter house had become a home. The couple had become a family. And, their two kids, who had grown up building castles and carving their names into the sand, were now off chasing their own dreams. And now, with their home a little quieter and professional life beginning to slow down, retirement had started to drift from a someday concept to a very present question.

Then, a shift crashed upon them like an outside set on a foggy dawn patrol.

Tom learned his father had suddenly passed away.

The loss uncovered something significant that day—a reminder that life, even when lived well, is still finite.

Before long, Tom found himself buried in a flood of forms, documents, and decisions that might have rivaled in size to his custom single-fin, 9-foot longboard. As anyone who's settled a loved one's estate knows, the process can test your patience like few other experiences on earth. However, what this process fostered was a sense of self-reflection, urgency, and a question he and Stacy hadn't fully dared to ask:

What is next for us and what are we waiting for?

Stacy was already retired, but Tom had the luxury of making work optional. He only worked because he wanted to, not because he felt he had to. Because he simply kept getting paid to do the research he loved, Tom never stepped back to ask himself the critical retirement questions.

As his perspective began to transform like a turning tide, Tom confided in a friend who happened to be a client of our firm. He talked with Stacy and they decided to schedule a call with us. During that first conversation, it was evident he and Stacy had put a lot of thought into what they were looking to get from financial planning and they were hoping our team would be a perfect fit for their goals.

We began our conversation by asking them about what they wanted their next chapter to look like. They had no initial visions of grandeur; they were primarily interested in knowing they had enough savings. Our team knew almost instantly that these two would be amazing to work with.

They were quite simply happy with the life they had built together, something we deeply admired.

As they onboarded with our firm, our analysis of their finances gave them the positive affirmation they so rightfully deserved. They had never done an analysis like this before. Throughout their lives, Tom and Stacy had simply operated as though they were still "living like grad students," believing that if they kept at it for a while and pretended like their pensions were just icing on the cake, everything would work out. And work out it did.

Coming to the realization they would likely be making more money in retirement than they did when they were working had them feeling like they were getting barreled on an otherwise choppy, knee-high day. But that wave turned out to be just the start of a long set and they now found themselves stuck in the churning whitewash.

As they looked further ahead, more questions began to surface—the kind they hadn't faced before. How do we navigate taxes? Is it costing us more if Tom continues working? Should we have delayed Stacy's pension? Is it hurting us to stay in CA?

We assured Tom and Stacy that the technical questions would be the easy part. The real questions for them to answer would be centered around what to do with all of this money.

For Tom and Stacy, these were uncharted waters. Those who can save a couple million dollars are often not the ones who can spend a couple million dollars. Our team challenged them to bring us as many dream scenarios as possible, and we would map out plans to maximize their potential.

Could they really take a chunk out of the nest egg they'd spent 30 years carefully building? Could they ultimately give themselves permission to use what they'd saved?

That question lingered—in their planning meetings as well as in quiet moments at home. That, more than anything else, was the roadblock.

They're not alone in that.

We've seen it time and again where people spend their working years sacrificing, saving, and deferring. And when the time comes to spend—to truly enjoy the fruits of those efforts—the muscle just isn't there. Dipping into savings that took an entire career to accumulate can feel reckless, even when the numbers say otherwise.

After two years of evolving conversations and countless modeled scenarios, they brought to us perhaps the wildest idea of all. What if they closed the mile-long gap between themselves and the beach? The thought of being able to walk to the beach had taunted them for years. They were close enough to enjoy everything the area offered but far enough that fighting traffic and parking problems were the norm.

The idea still felt indulgent—maybe even out of reach—but they couldn't shake it. That's when they called us again, this time with a bigger question. Could this dream ever become a reality? During our next meeting, we viewed their plans from multiple angles. While we proved that their plan had a lot of buffer, it still had its limits. A goal so ambitious would require careful planning, firm spending limits, and some unique financing and tax considerations.

We reviewed drawdown strategies from their investments, created a cash reserve, and their realtor helped them secure some equity financing to give them some additional liquidity and options. We worked through tax implications, what-if scenarios, future increases to fixed costs, and the long-term effects of reducing their investable assets. Every planning step was methodical, deliberate.

We didn't take the decision lightly—and neither did they.

With a plan limit set, the next step was finding the right home. Their budget was firm and their search area narrow, but their timeline gave them room to wait for the right opportunity.

Over the next year, Tom and Stacy would see many listings come and go. Like a set of waves passing under them in the line up, they paddled for some but had yet to find themselves in a position to take off and ride the glassy face.

And then one afternoon, it happened.

They found the best listing yet—weathered, a little dated, but perfectly imperfect with an ocean view and sunlight everywhere. We had helped them review a handful of listings over the last year, but the way they gleamed with enthusiasm made this one different. This one wasn't just another house. It had true potential to be their next home.

As the old adage goes, "Luck is where preparation meets opportunity."

All of our conversations up to this point, both the fun ones and the technical ones, had prepared them to move quickly and decisively at this very moment. As seasoned surfers know, you don't catch the wave of the day without first being in the right position to paddle. And paddle their hearts out they did!

Their offer was accepted. It has since blossomed into their perfect seaside bungalow. One that they continue to fix up and make their own. For Tom, he has fulfilled the lifelong dream of any surfer; he can walk his board a couple of blocks down the road and paddle out. For Stacy, she can do the same for an afternoon swim or for some artful inspiration. Their dog has been spoiled in all of this too. He gets daily walks on the beach, something I'm certain he lets his inland doggie pals know all about.

As financial planners, we're often paid based on the amount of money we manage—which makes decisions like this especially delicate. When a client withdraws a large portion of their portfolio, it means less revenue for the firm. That's just the reality of how many advisors are compensated. And yes, in a different planning relationship, someone might have nudged them away from a move like this.

But here's the thing: our job isn't to grow our bottom line, it's to help clients maximize the lives they've worked tirelessly to build. Tom and Stacy trusted us to help guide them toward the achievement of a cherished goal. In these situations, when we've been fortunate enough to build a deep, trusting relationship with our clients, decisions like this don't feel like a revenue loss. They feel like wins for everyone involved.

They didn't buy this house because they wanted to be flashy. They bought it because it made them feel more like themselves. It wasn't about square footage or property appreciation. It was about alignment—alignment with values, with passions, with the kind of life they envisioned when they were just starting out so many years before.

Buying a beach house in San Diego isn't the most relatable story. Not everyone wants that. Not everyone can afford it. But for Tom and Stacy, this was never about a beach house. It was about realizing their dream.

I suppose everyone has their beach house…

Maybe it's retiring two years earlier than planned, taking that trip to the Amalfi Coast, helping a child buy their first home, donating to a charity, starting a new business, building a cabin in the woods, restoring a vintage car, going back to school, moving closer to family, spending winters somewhere warm, or taking a break from work to write the book you've been quietly writing in your head for 20 years.

Whatever it is—that is your beach house.

And in our experience, most people don't give themselves the chance to go after it. Not because they can't, but because it's hard to shift from saving to spending—especially when the dream sounds too big or too bold. The fear of making a financial mistake in retirement can be paralyzing. The idea of taking from the safety net—the years of sacrifice it took to build and security it represents—can feel irresponsible, even selfish.

But if not now, when?

The truth is, your financial plan is more than a pie chart or a withdrawal rate. It's a reflection of your values, your hopes, your story. It's not just about numbers—it's also about giving you the confidence to live the life you've always imagined.

Tom and Stacy wrestled with their fair share of doubts and fears along the way. But ultimately, they were ready to boldly pursue a dream that was three decades in the making—no longer someday, but now.

They had made the long, steady paddle outside the break and found themselves perfectly positioned to catch the wave of their lifetime!

REFLECTIVE QUESTIONS

- What is your *beach house*? What dream or desire have you quietly set aside, thinking it might be too indulgent or out of reach?
- Have you given yourself permission to enjoy what you've worked so hard to build? If not, what beliefs or fears might be holding you back?
- If you knew you were financially secure, how would your life look different today? Would you live somewhere else, spend more freely, or reclaim time for something meaningful?

SUMMARY OF
MONEY IS FOR...
Dreaming

ACROSS EVERY STORY from this section, one truth emerges: money is not the dream, but it is the means by which dreams are made real.

Whether it's a baby longed for, a calling rediscovered, a plot of land nurtured over decades, or a long-awaited walk to the waves, each story reminds us that our financial lives are not separate from our deepest desires; they are intimately connected. Dreams ask us to act before the path is clear, to choose courage over certainty, and to believe that the future we imagine is worth planning for today.

When we align our resources with what matters most, money becomes more than a number. It becomes a tool for transformation. These stories demonstrate that with intention, creativity, and guidance, the dreams that once felt distant can become lived experiences.

So, what's your dream?

And what would it look like to start walking toward it—one choice, one dollar, one step at a time?

Because money is for dreaming.

And dreams are meant to be lived.

DESIGN YOUR FINANCIAL LIFE: MONEY IS FOR...
Dreaming

Identify *your* dream
☐ What would you do if money weren't an obstacle? Write it down in vivid detail.

What are you holding on to that keeps you from your dream?
Examples:
☐ Thoughts or beliefs about what "should" be
☐ Expectations of others for you
☐ Other property or financial commitments

Get specific: What are the numbers behind your dream?
Examples:
☐ Cost of property, interest rates
☐ Income changes
☐ Time frames
☐ Opportunity costs

Assess your resources (see Design Your Financial Life—Changing)

☐ Calculate the monthly cost of that dream

☐ Create a separate savings account and practice making payments toward it

☐ Consider how family members might contribute to your dream in non-traditional ways

Create small, meaningful steps

☐ Set a time frame to fulfill your dream

☐ What could you do this month to move closer to your dream?

☐ Who can hold you accountable to seeing your dream come true?

Find a guide

☐ Seek professional guidance to develop a realistic pathway to your dream

☐ Network with others who have achieved similar dreams to find practical solutions

☐ Get creative—brainstorm creative alternatives to traditional, costly services

MONEY IS FOR...
Giving

As we have discussed, money is about more than just spreadsheets and bank accounts. It reflects our values and identities. So, if living is the flame, and dreaming is the spark that ignites it, then giving is the light we cast into the world.

This section explores what happens when we stop asking "Will I have enough?" and start asking "What can I do with what I have—now?" Giving is often framed as a final act, something we leave behind. But the following stories remind us that the most powerful giving happens in the present, when we can look someone in the eye, offer help, and feel the joy ripple outward in real time.

These are not stories about grand gestures or press releases. They are quiet, generous acts—born from legacy, love, and sometimes, loss. They show us that giving isn't about what's left over. It's about showing up fully, while we still can. Whether it's helping a child breathe easier, a cause to thrive, or a family feel seen and supported, these stories echo a more profound truth: the greatest gift isn't the money itself—it's the presence, the trust, and the belief that something good can still be done.

Because when we give while we're still here to witness the impact, we don't just create change—we create connection. We give others a chance to flourish, and ourselves a chance to feel the sacred satisfaction of a life lived outward.

And in that, we find a wealth beyond measure.

FROM FEAR TO JOY: A JOURNEY OF GIVING

Emily Rassam, CFP®, CRPS®, CDAA, NSSA
Archer Investment Management

THE MOMENT I knew something had changed for Julia came in the form of a voicemail from her son.

"Hey Emily, it's Tom. Mom seems to feel different about money lately. She told me she's going to be fine. Then, for the first time ever, she gave each of us $5,000 at Christmas. She's even picking up the tab at dinner sometimes, which was a big surprise. I just wanted to thank you. Whatever you've done to help shift how she thinks about money has made a real difference."

It wasn't just an update; it was proof of something I had spent years hoping for. His mother, Julia, had spent her entire life clutching her money tightly, fearing that letting go, spending too freely, and giving too generously, was dangerous. To her, financial security meant control. And control meant never parting with a dollar unless it was necessary.

That mindset didn't change overnight.

A LIFE OF HOLDING ON

Julia had always been careful with money. She shared that she was raised by parents who lived through the Great Depression. She grew up with a clear message: money is tight, we don't have enough, and you must work hard for every penny you have. Later, when she married, she and her husband built their life from the ground up, priding themselves on being responsible, disciplined savers.

They were never reckless with money, but they were always waiting for "someday" when they'd feel more secure. Someday, they would fix up his classic car, which he dreamed of restoring but never quite got around to. Someday, they'd take more weekend trips to the beach instead of worrying about gas prices or hotel costs. Someday, they would feel ready to enjoy the wealth they had worked so hard to build.

But someday never came.

Her husband passed away five years ago, leaving Julia with everything they had saved but no one to enjoy it with.

By the time I met Julia, she was financially set for life. We ran the numbers every which way, and no matter how conservatively I projected her future expenses—healthcare, taxes, long-term care— she had more than enough to sustain her needs. But logic didn't stand a chance against the deeply ingrained fear in her mind.

Her reluctance wasn't just about money. It was about control. And more than anything, it was about avoiding the fate of an old family friend who had run out of money in retirement. That friend had retired early, spent freely, and had no pension to rely on. When the money ran out, he was forced to move in with family, becoming exactly what Julia feared most: a burden.

The irony was that Julia's financial picture was the complete opposite. She had a pension. She had savings. She had resources. But she couldn't shake the belief that one wrong move could send her down the same path.

Even while collecting Social Security and a pension, Julia kept saving. She didn't spend her required minimum distributions (RMDs); they just moved over to a different account, untouched. Even the money the IRS required her to withdraw she couldn't bring herself to use. I once asked her how much she thought she needed in savings to feel secure. She couldn't answer. There was no magic number. Just an ever-present, lingering fear of not enough.

PLANTING THE SEEDS

Over the years, I gently introduced the idea of giving. Not just through estate planning—though we covered that too—but while she was alive, when she could witness the impact firsthand.

"What if," I suggested, "you gave a little now as an experiment? Just small gifts to your children. See what it feels like…?"

She shook her head. "They're all successful; they don't need it."

Her kids were all financially stable. They were savers like her—people who reused wrapping paper, patched old jackets instead of buying new ones, and got excited about turning leftovers into three different meals. She didn't see the point in handing them money they hadn't asked for or "didn't need."

But I knew that wasn't the real issue.

The idea of voluntarily reducing her nest egg, even slightly, made her uneasy. It wasn't that she didn't want to give. She just didn't think she could without putting her own security at risk.

So, we reviewed her projections.

I mapped out different variables—what-ifs, worst-case scenarios, and every possible expense she could face. And when I showed her what her financial picture looked like in each case, there was no denying it: she wouldn't run out of money. She even said, "That's way too much" when looking at the estimated future value of her estate.

That's when I decided to be blunt. "Julia, if you wait until your kids inherit this money, they'll be in their 60s. They could be retired themselves by then. What if you gave a little now when they can actually use and enjoy it with their young families?"

I wasn't trying to pry money out of her hands. Just a nudge—an experiment.

One day, she paid for her family's dinner outing. Not by accident, not out of obligation, she just did it. Each family typically covered their own meals. A week later, she handed her granddaughter $20 for gas money. "She didn't ask," Julia told me. "I just thought it would be nice."

Her granddaughter was stunned and grateful. That simple moment lit Julia up in a way a bank account balance never could.

Little by little, she was loosening her grip.

A REFLECTION ON WHEN MONEY MATTERS MOST

One day, I asked Julia to reflect on her life and consider when a financial gift would have been most meaningful. She grew quiet, then shared a story I could tell still carried weight.

She was in her late 20s, standing in the checkout line at the grocery store with her three young children, when she realized she didn't have enough money to pay for everything in her cart. She had to take items out of her cart with other shoppers and the cashier watching. "That moment was awful," she admitted. "I felt so much shame. My face was burning, my hands were shaking, and I wanted to disappear. I remember the cashier glancing at the line behind me. It felt like everyone was watching."

In her 30s, she and her husband were managing better, but a financial gift would have meant feeling safe to buy new clothes for her growing kids, maybe even ones that weren't hand-me-downs for once. It would have covered sports fees and music lessons, things that always felt like a stretch but that they prioritized for their kids.

By her late 40s, money had stabilized more, but she and her

husband still had to make tough choices. Their kids had to pay their way through college with as much support as they could provide, but it wasn't enough to cover everything. "We did what we could," she said, "but there were limits. We didn't want to jeopardize our own security."

In their 50s and 60s, retirement decisions loomed. Could they afford to stop working when they wanted? A well-timed gift could have meant more confidence in that transition and fewer worries about whether they had saved enough.

And then, at 73, her husband passed. As she went through their finances, she kept uncovering more money. But by then, it didn't feel the same.

I asked her if there was anything she thought her kids long for but maybe don't have the money to prioritize at the moment—something a financial gift now could give them. She nodded. "They want to enjoy their kids while they're home now. They probably already have enough for retirement."

THE MOMENT EVERYTHING CHANGED

While finalizing her estate plan, Julia chuckled and said, "Well, I guess they should have some of it now."

That Christmas, she followed through.

She sat down, wrote three checks, $5,000 for each of her children, and tucked them under the tree.

When she told me, I held my breath. "How did that feel?"

She hesitated, then laughed. "Honestly? I thought I was going to be sick when I wrote the checks. But then I saw their faces when they opened them, and…" She exhaled and smiled, "we all cried."

Her children were stunned. Julia had never been a lavish gift-giver. Her presents were practical—socks, a book she thought they'd like, and maybe a gift card to their favorite restaurant. But this? This was different.

Her youngest daughter used the money for a family vacation to Disney. Tom put it toward a new front porch on his home. The third, a cautions saver tucked it away in her savings account like her mom.

Julia didn't care how they used it. And, that wasn't the point of the experiment.

A NEW KIND OF SECURITY

After Christmas, Julia made another change. She added two charities as payees on her account. She told me she planned to start making Qualified Charitable Distributions next year, where she'd directly contribute money from her IRA to charity.

"This feels good," she admitted. "They can use the money now."

She had spent her entire life believing that financial security came from holding tight, from never letting go. But now she understood something different: true security came from knowing she had "enough" and being able to use her money for something meaningful. She wasn't just accumulating wealth—she was enriching the lives of her family and the causes she cared about.

Dolly Parton once said, "Money is like manure. It's not worth a thing unless it's spread around, encouraging young things to grow."

Julia finally saw it, too. She enjoyed seeing photos of her grandchildren at Disney and felt proud sitting on the new front porch at Tom's home.

For the first time in her life, money wasn't just numbers on a page. It was love. It was connection. It was creating memories instead of regrets.

She would tell anyone now: "An old dog can learn new tricks."

And in the end, giving had made her feel richer than saving ever had.

REFLECTIVE QUESTIONS

- At which point in someone's life do you think a financial gift is most meaningful or useful?
- If someone looked at how you use money, what would they say you value most?
- Who in your life could use support—but hasn't asked for it?
- What's something you wish someone had given you earlier in life?
- What moment in your past would've changed everything—if someone had stepped in to help?
- Is there joy you're postponing until you feel "ready"?

Information in this story is presented is for educational purposes only. It should not be considered specific investment advice, tax advice, estate planning advice, or financial planning advice. It does not take into consideration your specific situation, and does not intend to make an offer or solicitation for the sale or purchase of any securities, planning, or investment strategies.

GIVING LIKE GOLDILOCKS

Justin Peek, CFP®, CCFC, CLTC®, AAMS®
PEEK WEALTH

EILEEN CARTER FELT herself panicking. And it wasn't because she and Helen were currently being subjected to another one of Barb's 'woe-is-me' tirades. No, something else was causing this. It began as a pit in her stomach a little earlier when Helen was telling them about another vacation she'd taken.

What had Helen said to trigger this discomfort? It wasn't that it was her third big trip already this year, though it was only June. And it wasn't that it was a lavish Safari, though Africa was on her bucket list too. Nor was it that Helen had paid for all 17 members of her family, including flights. None of that bothered Eileen. She was happy for her best friend.

Eileen's thoughts were halted when Barb set her drink down with an audible thud. "Eileen, what do you think of that? Are you even listening to me? Isn't that just terrible?"

"What? Yes, I mean. Of course that's awful. I'm sorry, you poor thing." Eileen had no idea what Barb had been complaining about. Her autoreply was a default these days to almost anything Barb said. Barb had aged 'sourly'—as she and Helen called it. Everything was a problem. Everyone was a problem. And Barb magically had all the answers.

That was it! It was Helen's comments about aging.

It was when she responded to Barb's accusation that she was spoiling her family with the Safari. Spoiling was something Barb made clear she and her family did *not* do after they sold their family business for many millions. And Barb made sure everyone knew just how much they received, and the amount of taxes they were "forced" to pay.

It was Helen's comments about time. She was telling them that they weren't getting any younger and that time isn't moving with them, it's moving *at* them, both uncontrollably and unpredictably. That was the moment this feeling had begun. Helen had mentioned an exercise her financial advisor had led her through with a meter stick and blue painters' tape which made her realize how little time she had left.

Eileen took control of the conversation and steered it back to Helen, "Hey Helen, what changed for you? Back when you had that session with your advisor. What was it specifically?"

Helen was beaming, "I'm telling you—it was so simple and mind-opening. Ok, so you can only be one of a couple of conditions in life, financially speaking. And…"

"Oh, here we go." Barb chirped, "Yes. Rich and poor. We all know."

"No. Stop it, Barb. Let me explain." She continued, "I know you're going to think I'm nuts, but when I was shown that I might only have '11 centimeters' left of my life at its best…"

Helen described her experience of the advisor's exercise and the questions which had intentionally created space for her to realize just how fast time was flying by. She said it awoke an immediate desire in her to do more. To give more. And it wasn't just in ways Eileen expected like updating estate plans or giving away larger amounts of money at death.

Surprising to Eileen, it was entirely about who Helen loved, what she loved, and why she loved. It became apparent to Helen that in the 'busyness' of her life, she'd lost track of the most important thing… time. She seemed to have plenty of it each day, yet by the end of each year, she wondered where it had all gone. She and Frank were guilty of playing the 'one day' game. One day, they'll do this or that. And 'this or that' wasn't just not happening, it had entirely been forgotten. It was no longer identifiable.

Barb was now scrolling her social feeds, clearly uninterested. Eileen, however, was identifying with Helen and asked, "So, then what, Helen? What did you do next?"

Helen reached forward and grabbed three sugar packets out of the plastic container in the center of the table and lined them up neatly in front of her. "So, before I did anything, I was taught something that's stuck with me. Let me show you."

Helen proceeded to carefully tear off the top of the first and third packets, leaving the packet in the middle untouched. Very carefully, she tipped out most of the first packet into the third, leaving just a little in one and overfilling the other.

"Careful." Eileen smiled.

"No, that's okay. That's the 'too much' one, it's supposed to spill over." Helen replied.

She continued, "Frank and I felt like we'd spent our whole lives petrified that we were a 'not enough'. That we didn't have the means to live the life we really wanted to. We held back, lived smaller for fear we'd run out. You've seen it, fewer trips, shorter trips. Less help to the family. We felt our resources were so limited and we had best be careful. 'Not enough' comes with fewer freedoms, right? Fewer choices. More stress. Less to spend, more to save, more money you need to make, all that."

Barb couldn't resist, "And there'd be fewer 'not enoughs' if people just learned to spend less! If you ask me, you can never have too much set aside. I'd rather die with millions in the bank than risk running out—or worse, giving it away too soon."

Helen turned to Barb, her smile widening, "What a wonderful intro to the 'too much's', thanks, Barb!" Barb rolled her eyes.

"Seriously, take a look at this third packet," Helen picked it up, more sugar grains falling out of it. "There's too much sugar in here, right? No different to someone having an overabundance of money. And I don't believe there's too much one can have, yet I believe there is too much that one can die with. We were raised to think that it's all about making the most, saving the most, and then passing it on to kids or charities. And, yes, we've made plans to leave what we want to those we care about. Yet, leaving is just not our priority, giving while we're still here is our guiding light now. And the funniest part, everyone we've increased our giving to happens to be those we love the most and were going to leave it to anyway! We just get to be a part of it."

Barb shifted uncomfortably and chimed in, "Oh great, so now you're going to just go spend everything you and Frank have saved and invested for without care for tomorrow? Is that what all these trips are about? What if you need that money later? What if one of you gets sick? And what kind of financial advisor is encouraging all this? Don't ever give me his card, nope, no thanks."

"Whoa! Come on Barb, that's not fair. You don't know our money situation. In fact, we're 'just right's' that never knew it. But think about what you literally just said, 'everything we've saved and invested for'. That's the point. Do you even know what that is for you, Barb?"

Barb sat upright, "Absolutely. A comfortable retirement for me and Steve and a division of our assets for our children once we pass. A little left to our church and university."

"Just. Like. That. So dull, Barb. Come on, we know you so well! What about the art school you dreamed of opening? Painting kept you sane throughout your career. What about your kids and grandkids? You've told us you see them maybe once a year?" Helen peppered her.

"They know where we are, we can't possibly afford to fly out there every time, now can we?"

"Can't you, Barb?" Helen challenged. "You know I love you, but you're not getting any younger. Get that art school open! Visit your family! Go mentor law students at the university and shape the careers of the next Barbara Blackthorns following behind you!" Barb appeared to briefly smile.

Helen picked up the middle packet of sugar. "All right, let me wrap this up because we need to start talking about your birthday, Eileen!"

"That's ok, please keep going, I love this!" Eileen relaxed back in her chair. Her earlier panic was now a growing excitement. Whatever this was that Helen was going through, Eileen wanted some too.

"Look at this perfect packet. Measured precisely. Nicely protected. It's 'just right' and that's what Frank and I discovered we are—financially speaking. Through all their crazy analytics and stress-testing, our advisor has assured us that not only can we do the things we hoped to be able to do comfortably, we're even able to do a lot more and not have any negative impact to us financially."

Eileen leaned back in. "Like?"

"All right, this makes me so happy. You know Maddie stopped working when her first child was born, right? Well, she loved her career and now with the whole world gone remote, I'm watching her kids for a half-day three days per week so she can consult and get a new business up and running! On top of that, Frank and I are taking the load off of some of the legal set up, helping them get their estate plan and insurances in place, this way her husband, Ryan, isn't further stressed."

"That's fantastic, how did you know she wanted this?" Eileen asked.

"I just asked! Our kids' generation are so much more in tune with their feelings and much better at expressing them too. So, at the advice of my advisor, I made myself uncomfortable and vulnerable for a minute and just asked Maddie and Ryan. I said, if Frank and I could help you in some way, monetary or otherwise, with no promise that we'd be able to, what could we do for you if you had a magic wand?"

"They didn't ask for a million dollars?" Barb's joke fell flat. "I'm kidding." She quickly followed up.

"Nope, but she intends to make a million dollars!"

"What else are you doing now?" Eileen asked.

"On the money side of things, we did do all the boring stuff and updated estate plans—our financial planner provides those services now—and we give more money to charity each year, especially after we were given expectations for how our portfolio will perform over time. We were way, way too conservative in our investments. And we're learning about the reality of taxes. Holy cow. If you're not doing conversions or whatever they're called… Anyway, you've seen the trips, and we have several more planned for just Frank and me."

"And what about Frank, what does he think of all this?" Barb asked.

"I think he needed this the most actually. He always made more than me and that stress of being the primary earner never goes away—it probably got worse for him once he stopped working. Yet with all the revelations we've experienced, he's all-in. He can truly let go of that feeling of sole responsibility. He's gone and joined the Carlsbad Charitable Foundation here in town and is applying all his years in sales to growing their membership. His goal is to double what the organization gives to charities each year. His former stress is literally a new source of strength for him."

Eileen, Helen, and Barb stayed another hour or so to discuss Eileen's birthday plans. And as Eileen walked back to her car, she was very eager for the conversation she was going to have with her husband, Ted. Helen had given her the very best gift someone could give, the gift of perspective and intention. Eileen's excitement bubbled up as she tucked Helen's advisor's card into her purse. She wondered how many 'centimeters' at her best she might have left as she clicked the key fob and opened the car door.

REFLECTIVE QUESTIONS

- Which sugar packet are you—too little, too much, or just right? How might you find out and how will you use that insight?
- Considering who and what you love (and who loves you), how can you give more of your time, skills, or financial resources?

Thank you for reading my story, with so many in here, that means a lot. I wrote it myself with no use of AI or ghostwriting, so it's an 'original', if you will. And that is exactly how we provide financial planning and manage investments for you—authentic, personal, and crafted just for you. My firm and team at PEEK WEALTH practices Lifestyle Financial Advising, inspired by the financial planning philosophy of Paul Armson. To discover what we might be able to do for you, you are welcome to email me at info@peekwealth.com. And regarding our client community and my team serving them, I assure you it's all Helens and Eileens with no Barbs in sight! It's a peaceful place where some really incredible financial advising takes place. You can check us out or read about actual client experiences here: www.peekwealth.com.

CREATING AN ENDURING LEGACY

Cleve Gantt, CFP®, M.S.
Gantt Financial Advisors

T HE STORM BLEW up out of nowhere—summer thunderstorms in the Gulf often do. One minute, the sea had been a shimmering playground, the boat rocking on a light chop. The next, eight-foot swells were slamming into the hull and sending sprays of saltwater across the deck.

Mark glanced around at the fishermen. Just minutes ago, they'd been grinning like kids, reeling in red snapper, cobia, triggerfish, and grouper. Now, the laughter had vanished. In its place were tight jaws, wide eyes, and white knuckles. They were 40 miles offshore, deep in the Gulf, and it was obvious none of them had faced a storm like this before.

But Mark had.

At 17, he was just the deckhand—working under his dad, the captain—but these trips had shaped him more than any classroom ever could. It wasn't just about baiting hooks or untangling lines. It was about watching for needs before they were spoken. About steadying others when the wind picked up and the skies turned dark.

And Mark loved it.

Mark embraced the fact the Gulf could change from calm to

chaos in a breath. He loved helping friends have the time of their life, creating memories for a lifetime.

For Mark, this became more than just a summer job.

This was where Mark was learning what it meant to lead by serving—how to be calm when others panicked, how to bring peace just by being present.

And somewhere between the laughter and the lightning, Mark fell in love with the quiet strength that came from putting others first.

Decades later, that same strength was about to be tested in a different way—yet in many ways similar.

The storm this time wasn't on the water. It was brewing beneath the surface, harder to see, but just as fierce.

As Mark and Lisa waited for the doctor to walk into the room, they passed the time talking about their plans for the summer, and spending time with their son, Jim, and his family in Atlanta. Mark had had some unusual symptoms recently, but didn't think they amounted to anything serious. But when the door swung open and the doctor walked in, they sensed the seriousness of this conversation.

The doctor took a deep breath and sat down across from Mark and Lisa, his eyes filled with quiet understanding. He folded his hands together, leaning in slightly, his voice calm but gentle.

"Mark, I know this isn't the news you were hoping for. We've run extensive tests, and they indicate you have Amyotrophic Lateral Sclerosis, known as Lou Gehrig's disease. It's a slow-moving disease, and while we can't predict the exact timeline, most people in your situation live anywhere from three to five years."

"I want you to know, though, that you are not alone in this. We'll be with you all the way and provide treatment and support that will help you maintain a good quality of life as long as possible.

Mark reached for Lisa's hand, his grip firm despite the weight of the news. "Lisa, we're not going to let this disease define us," he said, his voice steady but full of feeling.

"We're going to treasure every moment we have, and we're going to live every single day we have to its fullest."

Lisa wiped her tears and looked into his eyes, "Mark, you've always faced life with courage, and I'll be right here beside you—every step of the way."

That night, as they sat on the porch in silence, struggling to absorb the news, Mark finally spoke. "Lisa, I won't lie—this won't be easy. Not for me, not for you. Or for Jim and his family."

Lisa squeezed his hand. "Mark, I know this is overwhelming and scary, but I also know you. If anyone can turn this into a victory, it's you."

Mark took a deep breath. "Lisa, our lives on earth may be like a vapor, but we can still make an eternal difference through the way we live the time we have, and the resources God has entrusted to us. That's what's important to me now, more than ever."

A LEGACY IN MOTION

Mark was a person of deep faith. For Mark, money was never the goal—only a tool to serve a greater purpose. His perspective made things like legacy and relationships more important than profits. Mark believed he came into this world without any material things, and that he would leave the world without any material things. Mark's view was he was just the temporary steward of his financial resources.

Mark was 73 years old when he received the news. He had retired as a charter boat captain at age 70 but still managed the marina where his old boat was now leased to a younger captain.

Mark and Lisa married late in life, and Jim was their only child. A very successful attorney in Atlanta, Jim was married with two children.

While Mark was very generous, he also knew the importance of saving.

During the time I worked with Mark as his financial advisor, his business became more profitable, and we looked at ways to be more tax efficient. Because Mark was self-employed, we set up a solo 401(k) plan that allowed him to put away a significant portion of his salary on a tax deferred basis. Mark liked to keep things simple and consistent. He learned about the power of global diversification of a portfolio and that trying to spend time outguessing the investment markets was fruitless. As a result, Mark's 401(k) was worth just a little over $3.5 million when he retired at 70. When Mark retired, he rolled his 401(k) over to a traditional IRA.

PLANNING WITH PURPOSE

When Mark and Lisa came to the office for the first time after receiving the news, Mark began sharing his heart and goals. "I know this life is finite for all of us. I want the time I have left to make a difference, not only for my family, but for those who are less fortunate than me. I've always looked at life as a gift—every sunrise, every breath, every moment with the people we love. I would like to create a framework for a legacy that lasts well beyond my life, and even beyond the lives of my grandchildren.

My priority is to make sure Lisa is well taken care of with enough income for her to live comfortably the rest of her life. I think we need to sell the marina because it's too much for Lisa to manage, and Jim already has a successful career. Besides that, I want to teach my grandchildren how our material resources can impact this world for good. I want to leave this world a better place than I found it."

PLANNING WITH HISTORY IN MIND

Mark's dad had taught him how to fish and handle a boat. It was no wonder Mark developed a deep love for entrepreneurship, but also for fishing. Mark's dad recognized these traits in Mark, and his parents left the marina to him after they passed away.

Mark's dad needed extensive care before he passed away. As executor for his parents, Mark had witnessed the gradual drain on their estate because there wasn't enough cash flow to cover the expenses of care for his dad. This left Mark's mom in a precarious financial position.

Not long after Mark's dad passed away, he asked me about being prepared should he or Lisa have such a problem toward the end of their life. Mark said, "I don't want to put a burden on Lisa, and I sure would like to be independent and taken care of comfortably in my own home". Initially Lisa was dismissive of the need for such precautions, but Mark won her over by explaining that they could free up a lot of their own assets if they let an insurance company provide the needed capital to pay for expenses, rather than save up a lot of money earmarked just for a health contingency. This would allow them to share the risk of a health change with many others, for the price of a premium.

When the news came of Mark's illness, such a decision appeared to be prescient.

PLANNING FOR GENERATIONS

As our discussion went on, we considered what to do about the marina and Mark's reasoning behind selling it. I explained the first step was getting an appraisal from a Certified Valuation Analyst for the business, in addition to a real estate appraisal for the property.

After we received the results of the appraisals, we learned that the marina and property had appreciated in value exponentially since Mark had inherited it from his parents. Selling the marina and the property now would result in massive long-term capital gains taxes.

Mark didn't want to leave Lisa with the task of selling the marina and property, and he expressed surprise and concern to me about the dilemma posed by the problem from the long-term capital gains taxes.

As our discussions continued, we began to work on a potential solution.

After we discussed several different options, Mark and Lisa settled on a plan that would not only reduce their tax burden but also ensure their wealth served a greater purpose.

They started by creating a Limited Liability Company (LLC) and transferred the marina and real estate into it. From there, they carefully structured the proceeds from the sale to align with their goals.

Mark explained the plan to Lisa one evening over dinner. "Remember when we had the person who spoke at church about the tragic stories of children in Eastern Europe who were being exploited and trafficked? I would love to save as many of those children as we can. We're going to allocate 20% of the proceeds to a Donor-Advised Fund to support a charity that rescues children from human trafficking in Eastern Europe."

Lisa's eyes softened. "That's incredible, Mark. Your dad would be so proud."

Mark continued, "Then, we'll place 20% into a Dynasty Trust for the grandchildren. That way, they'll have a secure future, even long after we're gone."

Lisa nodded, listening intently.

"The biggest portion—60%—will go into a Charitable Remainder Unitrust, or CRUT," Mark said. "That's the part that ensures you have income for life. It also defers taxes, so we aren't hit with everything at once."

Lisa smiled, squeezing his hand. "So, we're not just avoiding taxes—we're making sure our money does something good."

"Exactly," Mark said. "And there's more. Since the CRUT contribution offers a tax deduction, I'll use that to partially offset the taxes on a Roth conversion and make Jim the beneficiary. That way, Jim won't get crushed by taxes when he inherits it. He's already in a high bracket."

Lisa leaned back in her chair, processing it all. "And what about the IRA?"

"You'll inherit that," Mark assured her. "You can use it for income just as if it were yours.

After you're gone, it'll go into a Testamentary Charitable Remainder Unitrust. That trust will provide income to the grandkids for 20 years, which is twice the usual ten years allowed by a Beneficiary IRA. At the end of 20 years, the remainder flows into the Donor-Advised Fund, which Jim and his children will oversee."

Lisa's eyes glistened with emotion. "So, the money keeps working—helping the family and supporting causes we care about."

Mark nodded. "That's the goal. I want to make sure you're secure, the grandkids have a strong future, and we teach the next generation of our family about the eternal impact we can have with our financial resources."

As they watched the sun set, Mark felt a deep sense of peace. His father had built the marina with hard work; now Mark was shaping a legacy to outlast it—a legacy not of buildings or boats, but of faith, generosity, and purpose.

Mark and Lisa understood that true wealth isn't measured by a balance sheet, but by the lives we touch and the eternal impact we make with what we've been given. Through thoughtful stewardship—trusts, charitable giving, and intentional planning—they could secure Lisa's future, strengthen their grandchildren's foundation, and ensure their resources would continue changing lives long after they were gone.

Mark and Lisa's story is a testament to the power of purposeful planning—showing that it can do more than sustain life; it can transform it.

Through their life and choices, Mark and Lisa left a legacy of faith, love, and hope—one that would endure for generations.

And that was a future worth planning for.

REFLECTIVE QUESTIONS

- How do I want my life and resources to make a difference?
- Have I taken the necessary steps—like creating a will, trust, or charitable plan—to ensure that my values, priorities, and loved ones are protected?

THE JOY OF (GIVING) NOW

Chris Magaña, MBA, JD

THIS STORY IS to honor a humble, reluctant hero, Jon. He led without trying, gave without asking, and taught without needing credit. For nearly 20 years, I witnessed it all as his financial advisor and, more importantly, a friend.

Jon and Shelly certainly had enough wealth to sustain them until ancient times. Their home held layers, two lives joined, with adult children on each side, two pots of money, and the quiet complexity of what that meant.

If there was a cause worth fighting for, Jon was already there: serving on boards, ringing bells, knocking on doors, and quietly holding his town together. You can still feel Jon's influence in every splintered playground bench, every crop harvested from a community garden, every diploma or GED proudly clutched in trembling hands at the local community college. Jon didn't just believe in community. He showed up for it, again and again. That's what I admired most: generosity lived in his bones.

A thoughtful strategy for his giving? That came later, with reflection and intention.

We would plot and scheme (for good causes) about different ideas, usually over gin and tonics. Jon was your classic, impulsive "ah shucks" giver. He didn't want the attention; he just wanted the giving to happen. He wanted the organizations he cared about deeply to have the money they needed to complete their important work.

Jon's CPA and attorney wanted the bulk of his charitable giving to happen upon his death via his estate plan. The attorney also wanted the bulk of his assets to be split between his children, his spouse after he passed, and some to charity. You could tell Jon was uneasy with this plan.

His professionals planned his legacy; Jon wanted to live it, see it, and be inspired by it while he could. Jon and I agreed that giving to his children (already in their 50s) and the community in his estate plan upon death wouldn't solve today's problems. Jon would say, "Money can make a real difference now." He knew his children might miss out on opportunities for growth and security that earlier financial gifts could provide.

Timing is crucial. Gifting money when your children can still actively use it to build their careers, start businesses, or buy homes can have a much more profound impact than waiting until you're gone.

Jon and I spent much time on the retirement spreadsheets, ensuring we didn't underestimate his future needs and that he could withstand multiple stock and bond downturns. The fear of running out of money is a legitimate concern. It did take some work, time, and analysis to determine "the number" Jon was comfortable giving. Jeopardizing his future was not an option, so we held back about 10% more wealth than was optimal on paper.

Having a margin of safety was essential to both Jon and me. Jon was notorious for stashing chocolate around the house for "emergencies". Similarly, to Jon's philosophy on stashing chocolate in case of a pinch, I believe that stashing some extra wealth creates the necessary margin of safety to have the confidence required to execute the generosity plan.

We opted to accelerate the giving strategy. We started meeting with community groups Jon cared about and started making financial commitments, followed by checks (these were actually appreciated stocks with low basis, which can be a much more tax-efficient way to give).

Three things happened that neither of us expected.

Firstly, Jon experienced a deepening of relationships and connection to others. His giving introduced him to other like-minded individuals. His base of friendships expanded. Many of these friendships he carried until his passing, providing several years of joy, laughs, and friendly competition about who could grow better tomatoes—Jon's heirloom tomatoes were so good that I would give him in-person weekly updates on his portfolio during tomato season. Sidebar: Weekly updates for buy-and-hold investors are largely pointless.

Some of these new connections now rank as Jon's widow Shelly's most trusted friends.

Secondly, these gifts allowed the talented nonprofit organizations to work their magic and inspire others to give more. They leveraged Jon's gifting as a financial challenge for others to match and subsequently accelerated the size of their savings and endowments. Jon heard firsthand from program managers, executive directors, and the nonprofit board what they planned to use his gifts for and how much these funds meant to them. Seeing these community groups multiply his gifts gave Jon great comfort in his final days. These stories continue to be shared and celebrated by Jon's family, galvanizing his legacy.

At the annual gala for one of the causes that Jon had quietly supported, his family still fills a table reserved in his honor. Before his passing, the cause felt like "dad's thing," something meaningful, but distant. Now, it's something more. The gala has become a gathering place for his beautifully blended family: a space to remember Jon, share stories, give updates, and, in their own quiet way, carry on his legacy. What began as Jon's personal mission is now a family tradition. They don't make headlines with their gifts, but they show up year after year to give, honor, and keep the spirit of Jon's giving alive.

Finally, on the personal side, Jon's decision to give sooner to his children made a huge difference in their lives. At the same time, both sons had their lives materially improved by their dad's generosity.

Wes, Jon's youngest son, has always been passionate about American muscle cars, which can be an expensive hobby. The early giving enabled Wes to purchase the 66 Mustang Fastback he had always wanted and "trick it out," just like Wes's 18-year-old self would have been proud of. Jon wasn't "a car guy," but they were able to bond over the progress on the car. Jon knew what that car meant to his son. Jon, not being a car guy, had to get over his gift being used to buy American muscle instead of an index fund. It took time for Jon to unclench, to stop second-guessing and start trusting the gift for what it was: love, not leverage.

Eventually, Jon realized that handing over wealth is about trust, respect, and love. It's about acknowledging that a person (or charity) can make choices and should be allowed to face the consequences, good or bad. This process is fundamental to personal growth and accountability. I believe Jon knew that if Wes didn't have the maturity and financial chops to handle this wealth in his 50s, would it be different in another ten or 15 years?

Giving now also meant that Cal, Jon's oldest son, was able to "slow down" at work and move to part-time, enabling him to be a more engaged and active parent to his son Jason.

In his signature blend of deep love and slightly off-color humor, Jon often referred to Cal (I hope proudly) half-jokingly as "the best soccer mom" Jason could ever have. Jason didn't have a game or practice that Cal didn't attend, armed to the teeth with orange slices, water bottles, and snacks, ready as ever.

It started as something simple: a dad with extra time, leaning into the little moments. But when the pandemic dismantled Jason's world—school disrupted, friendships fractured, sports gone, and a divorce which further cracked his foundation—Cal's presence stopped being nice to have. It became Jason's lifeline. What began as quality time became critical time.

Once a confident, social kid, Jason grew quiet and withdrawn, untethered by the chaos around him and unsure of where to place the pain.

Jon didn't see all the good his giving did—he was taken from us before the hard stuff hit Jason—but he got to see enough. In the end, Jon was thankful for giving when he did because it gave Cal the confidence and resources to slow down and be a hyper-engaged dad to Jason when he needed it most. I know Jon would be proud of Cal for making those choices. It's difficult to quantify the richness Jon created in his last seven to eight years which would not have existed had he not decided to give when he did.

There are a variety of lessons that can be learnt from Jon's experience of giving.

Accelerating his giving strategy allowed Jon to form deep connections and friendships with like-minded individuals in his community. These relationships enriched his life and continued to support Shelly after his passing.

Jeopardizing his financial future was not an option. Jon knew that doing the work upfront to get the "right number" to give was critical for his peace of mind and family harmony.

The decision to give sooner can be a bonding and connecting experience. Creating cherished memories and new interests and strengthening their relationship.

Gifting during your lifetime is more than a financial decision; it's about creating immediate value and impact. When you give now, you can guide, support, and witness the bounties of your treasure.

It can be uncomfortable to watch your family make choices you wouldn't, especially with the money you gave them. But that discomfort is part of the gift. Accept that their decisions won't be yours. That doesn't make them wrong.

Unlike hairlines or a tendency to stash chocolate (both Jon's sons do it as well), hobbies and passions aren't always inherited. You don't pass them down, so you take an interest in what interests them, whether your kids are 15 or 50.

And if you're still on the fence about giving now versus later, consider this: the helper's high is real. Giving has been linked to lower stress, greater happiness, a stronger sense of purpose, and even longer life. You don't just do good. You feel it.

It's one thing to be remembered. It's another thing to be there: to see the impact. To hear the laughter. To help carry the weight when life gets heavy.

Deathbed charity can be a cop-out. Love louder. Give sooner.

Or, as my Abuela says: "Give me flowers when I'm alive, not when I'm gone."

REFLECTIVE QUESTIONS

- What if the real legacy isn't in the money left... but in the moments made while you're still here to witness them?
- What joy am I postponing in the name of being "practical"?

SUMMARY OF MONEY IS FOR...
Giving

GIVING ISN'T JUST about generosity; it's about presence.

To give while we're here is to say: I see you now. I love you now. I trust you now.

In these stories, we've seen that giving isn't reserved for the wealthy or the end of life. It's available to all of us, in moments both grand and quiet. A check written with shaky hands. A legacy planned with care. A gift that rebuilds a porch or a relationship.

Each act of giving, whether to family, community, or a cause, became something more—a connection, a transformation, and a source of healing. Not one of these gifts waited until the reading of a will. They bloomed while the giver could still witness the joy, the relief, the impact.

Because the point isn't just to be remembered.

It's to remember ourselves, as someone who showed up with open hands and a full heart.

So give now. Give loudly or give quietly.

But give while you're here.

As the saying goes:

Bring me flowers while I'm alive, not when I'm gone.

DESIGN YOUR FINANCIAL LIFE: MONEY IS FOR... *Giving*

Discover your giving passion

☐ Record a voice memo reflecting on what moves you most deeply.

☐ Which people, causes, or organizations ignite your passion?

Share your vision

☐ Who in your life needs to know about your giving intentions?

☐ How will you communicate your giving philosophy to family, a spouse, or children?

☐ What conversations do you need to have to align your household around giving goals?

☐ How will you involve others in your giving journey?

Assess your giving capacity

☐ Time: How many hours per week/month can you realistically volunteer or engage?

☐ Talent: What unique skills, expertise, or connections can you contribute?

☐ Treasure: What percentage of income or specific dollar amount can you give annually?

☐ How might your capacity change over time as your life circumstances evolve?

Define your giving strategy
☐ Who do you want to benefit from your giving?
☐ When would your gifts have the greatest impact?
☐ Who do you hope to inspire by your example of giving?
☐ What legacy do you want your giving to create?

Explore giving tools and strategies
☐ Do you need technical giving solutions?
    ☐ Donor-advised funds for flexible, tax-efficient giving
    ☐ Charitable remainder trusts for income and tax benefits
    ☐ Direct giving versus planned giving strategies
☐ What are the annual giving limits and tax implications?
☐ Should you consider gifting appreciated assets instead of cash?

Consider the cost of inaction
☐ Imagine you never gave anything significant, whether money, time, or attention. Record a voice memo answering these questions:
    ☐ What opportunities to make a difference would you miss?
    ☐ How would you feel looking back on a life lived without intentional generosity?
    ☐ What impact would remain unmade if you chose not to give?
    ☐ How might this affect your sense of purpose and fulfillment?

MONEY IS FOR...
Enduring

Not everything in life can be planned.

Loss arrives uninvited. Illness alters the course. Promises are broken, dreams are delayed, and grief, in all its forms, comes asking who we really are beneath the surface.

In this section, we sit with stories that don't wrap up neatly. These are not tales of growth or gain—but of perseverance. Of navigating the hardest seasons. Of finding a way forward when the map disappears.

Here, money is not a tool for achieving but for enduring. It is for holding families together when a parent is gone, honoring a loved one lost too soon, bearing the weight of unexpected caregiving, and carrying on, day by day, when the plan you once trusted no longer applies.

But these stories also remind us: endurance is not just about survival. It's also about honoring what matters most in the face of what hurts the most. It's about choosing love when fear could easily take over. It's about using financial clarity to create space for healing, honesty, and hope.

Because when life breaks open, what remains is what's real: relationships, purpose, memory, and the sacred work of simply showing up.

Money can't take away pain. But it can soften the edges, create options, and give us room to breathe. It can't keep life from falling apart, but it can help us piece it back together, one act of care, one conversation, one decision at a time.

EVERYTHING EVERYWHERE ALL AT ONCE

Michal Skowronski, CFP®
Skylark Wealth

"An ounce of prevention is worth a pound of cure."
—Benjamin Franklin

A CALL IN THE NIGHT

S USAN'S PHONE LIT up on the kitchen counter, Paul's name flashing across the screen. It was late—her brother never called at this hour. A quiet unease settled in her chest, a feeling that this wasn't just a casual check-in.

She picked up, her voice cautious. "Hey, Paul?"

"Susan, it's me," he said, his voice clipped. "We need to talk…"

In that moment, her unease sharpened into dread. Whatever he was about to say, she knew in her gut it would turn her world upside down.

BEFORE THE STORM

Life had felt stable, almost predictable. Susan's biggest worries were a looming work project deadline and what to grab for dinner on her way home. Her father, Peter, seemed to be enjoying a carefree retirement, his savings, carefully grown over decades, secure enough to cover her daughters' graduate school tuition—a promise that eased her mind. Her own finances, shaped by careful planning with our firm, were solid. Her girls were thriving, wrapping up college with big plans. At the same time, Susan's brother Paul was adjusting to life as an empty nester after settling his freshman daughter into her dorm. Everything seemed on track. Until now.

THE DIAGNOSIS

"Dad's got Alzheimer's," Paul said, his voice heavy. "He can't live alone anymore."

Susan's breath caught. The words landed like a quiet earthquake, shaking the foundation of her world. Her father, always so sharp, so independent, a man who recited poetry and balanced checkbooks in his head—now this. Her mind spun with questions: Who'll care for him? Where? How?

She clung to one small relief: money wasn't going to be an issue. Peter's retirement savings, carefully built over decades, were enough to cover his care and her daughters' graduate school, just as he'd promised.

"There's no money," Paul said, cutting through her thoughts.

"What?" Susan's voice cracked. "How?"

Paul's sigh carried years of weight. "He lost it all. Day trading options on his portfolio. It's gone."

Susan's breath caught. The savings, their anchor, were gone. Her mind reeled: How could this happen?

THE WEIGHT OF LOSS

Paul's call struck Susan with quiet grief—Peter's Alzheimer's had him calling her "Mom," his mind unraveling. The squandered savings stung—a wound deepened by looming care costs and her daughters' threatened dreams. Anxiety churned—how would Alzheimer's reshape their family? Helplessness gripped her: no cure could restore Peter; no funds could be reclaimed from his reckless trades. Yet compassion stirred—she yearned to protect her vulnerable father.

Paul, equally adrift, scoured Alzheimer's forums, grasping at straws. He shared a care subsidy link, a small step. Their questions hung heavy: This can't be real. What now? Where's the money going to come from? Who'll care for him? Where will he live?

FINDING A PATH

For many, such a crisis demands desperate measures—slashing expenses, borrowing, or relying on unprepared loved ones stepping in. Susan, though, was prepared, not by foresight but by habit. Years of living within her means, consistent saving, and prudent investing with our firm, had built a resilient nest egg. These habits had armed her to endure—not because she foresaw this crisis, but because she was ready for the unknown. Only now did the shape of that endurance become clear: her savings would anchor her family through Peter's illness.

Where's the money? Peter's checking account held some funds, managed by Paul under a power of attorney from Peter's recently updated estate plan. Susan's robust retirement savings could bridge gaps. Peter's long-term care insurance, wisely purchased, covered key costs. They also explored other potential sources of income including state and local aid as well as Peter's health insurance and weighed-up in-home care versus assisted living.

Who'll care for him? Peter's estate plan clarified roles. A trust named Paul as successor trustee, granting access to remaining funds.

A healthcare directive empowered Paul to make decisions aligned with Peter's wishes, easing administrative burdens.

Where will he live? Susan wanted Peter nearby. Her stair-filled home, however, while charming, was impractical without costly changes. After tearful talks, she and Paul chose a nearby assisted living facility where Peter would be safe and accessible.

Healthy financial habits, prudent insurance, and an up to date estate plan didn't erase the pain but made the path that much more bearable.

THE NEW NORMAL

Paul, acting under Peter's power of attorney, managed his remaining accounts and budgeted Peter's assets for bills and care. They relocated Peter to an assisted living facility near Susan's home, coordinating his care with his doctor. The long-term insurance claim, initially denied, was approved after an appeal, easing the strain. Susan worked with us to allocate her savings wisely, ensuring tax-efficient support for Peter without derailing her daughters' future. Susan and Paul consulted a local elder care attorney to help navigate state and local resources.

Susan visited Peter often, holding his hand through moments of confusion, cherishing glimpses of his old smile. She and Paul grew closer, their shared burden forging a quiet strength.

A LESSON IN RESILIENCE

Susan's story of enduring ends with hope, but not without scars. Every day, many face life-altering moments—whether it's the sudden responsibility of caring for a loved one who can no longer manage alone, or challenges like a job loss, a bitter divorce, or an unexpected retirement. These moments bring grief, tough choices, and financial strain. Susan's foresight—her steady saving, her father's insurance, professional guidance, and her family's unity—eased her path. By planning today, you can create your own anchor, softening the blow of tomorrow's storms making it just that much easier to find a way to move forward when crisis strikes.

PREPARING FOR A CRISIS: KEY QUESTIONS AND STEPS

Imagine a phone call announcing that a loved one needs your support—emotional, financial, or physical. Be ready by addressing these questions and taking these steps:

1. **Who will provide care?** Identify who will step up—you, a family member, or professionals—and ensure they're prepared.
2. **Where will care be provided?** Choose the best setting, such as the loved one's home, your home, or a specialized facility, based on accessibility and needs.
3. **How will care be managed?** Plan the logistics, including financial resources, medical support, and legal arrangements, for sustainability.

ACTION STEPS TO PREPARE

For Money Management or Mental Decline:
- Engage a financial advisor: Partner with a professional to manage finances, especially if cognitive decline is a risk.
- Consult a local specialist: Work with an elder care attorney or social worker familiar with local resources to navigate care options and subsidies.
- Establish a power of attorney: Designate a trusted person to make financial and healthcare decisions if incapacity strikes.

For Financial Preparedness:

- Self-insure through savings: Allocate income or investments now to cover potential care costs for yourself or a loved one.
- Explore insurance options: Consult an insurance professional about private disability and long-term care insurance. Avoid relying solely on employer-provided coverage, which may lapse if employment ends.

For Legal and Estate Planning:

- Create or review an estate plan: Work with an estate planning attorney to establish or update wills, trusts, financial power of attorney, and healthcare directives for yourself and loved ones.
- Verify asset titling and beneficiaries: Ensure all assets (accounts, home, car, benefits, life insurance) have current titling and beneficiary designations to avoid delays or disputes.

REFLECTIVE QUESTIONS

- How prepared are you for the possibility that someone you love might need significant care or financial support from you?
- What financial safeguards do you have in place to protect yourself and your family from your own potential future incapacity?
- Are your "boring" financial protections, like long-term care insurance, disability coverage, and estate planning, as current and robust as your investment strategies?

MONEY IS FOR LEGACY: THE STORY OF JOHN AND HIS THIRD CHILD

Eric Nelson, CFP®, CEPA
Independence Wealth

THE MORNING BEGAN the way countless others had for John: quietly, with the smell of brewing coffee and the low hum of fluorescent lights in his office. Outside, the sun struggled against a thick New Jersey haze, but John barely noticed. His mind was already inside the day—customer issues, staffing shortages, the stubborn supplier he still hadn't heard back from.

This company wasn't just where John worked. It was who he was.

For nearly 40 years, he and his wife Diane had built it together, brick by brick. Their two children, Michael and Emily, had grown up in its shadow: Michael, always asking questions about the trucks, the inventory, the margins. Emily, seeming more fascinated by the wide world beyond the office walls.

Still, Diane often said the same thing whenever anyone asked about their life: "We have three children. Michael, Emily, and the business."

And yet for all that effort, for all that identity, succession planning had always been like trying to grab mist. Talked about, intended, but never settled. Too many variables. Too much heart involved.

What if Emily eventually wanted in? Would splitting things equally be fair? Would John ever truly feel ready to step back?

There was always another project, another customer, another year to figure it out.

Until the day the phone rang.

John had suffered a heart attack. Severe. Crushing. The kind that doctors describe clinically, but families experience in slow-motion horror. Paramedics, sirens, a helicopter ride John wouldn't even remember. Emergency surgery.

And then the waiting.

In a sterile hospital waiting room, under too-bright lights, Diane gripped a Styrofoam cup of coffee she couldn't bring herself to drink. Michael paced. Emily stared out the window, jaw tight, silent.

Everything they had built, everything they had avoided talking about, hung in the air like a fragile thread about to snap.

John survived. Against the odds, against the fear in the surgeons' eyes, he made it through. But the man who eventually returned home wasn't the same. His handshake was weaker. His voice, slower. His eyes, sharper in a way that suggested he saw something the rest of them didn't.

The time for "someday" was over.

Not long after coming home, he called me.

"It's time," John said, his voice scratchy but certain. "No more waiting."

We moved quickly. Legal documents. Governance structures. Defined roles. Ownership paths. Meetings that once had been theoretical were now urgent. Conversations that had once danced around emotions now wrestled with them head-on.

Michael would run the business. Officially, operationally, structurally.

For a time, there was a kind of grace to it. The business, finally released from its dependence on John's constant guidance, found new life under Michael's leadership. Clients noticed. Employees responded. Growth came faster than anyone predicted.

But even in growth, shadows linger.

Emily, from her own career in a different industry, felt a complex knot of emotions—pride, sadness, displacement. She didn't want to run the business, but she also didn't want to feel erased from the story.

Diane, struggled with how quickly Michael was asserting his leadership. Should she slow things down? Retain more control? Had they moved too fast, too soon?

Michael, feeling the weight of expectations and the limitations of partial ownership, pressed harder for clarity.

Tensions brewed quietly at first, then with a little more heat. Conversations that once glided along on trust now snagged on technicalities. Was the transfer happening too fast? Was Diane giving up too much? Was Michael owed more after carrying the business through a season of loss?

And then, without warning, came the second blow.

John suffered another medical event. This time, there was no helicopter. No surgery.

He passed away at home, surrounded by family, the faint smell of Diane's cooking in the kitchen.

The funeral was crowded, filled with faces from every chapter of their lives: employees, clients, neighbors, friends. Yet beneath the hugs and condolences, real fears gnawed at the family's foundations.

The business was growing. The opportunities were real. But the absence of John, the quiet gravity he had provided, left a vacuum. Without him, emotions began to pull the family in different directions.

Ownership questions that had been academic suddenly became urgent—and personal.

Diane, now the sole owner, found herself both empowered and burdened. Michael, running the company day-to-day, needed the authority and security of ownership to lead confidently. Emily, still distant from the business, quietly wondered if she mattered at all to the events unfolding.

I knew the only path forward was through—not around—the discomfort.

We set the meeting. Neutral ground. No office politics. No family home memories. Just a room with too many chairs, a whiteboard no one wanted to write on, and a clock ticking louder than it should have.

Everyone came in armored. Guarded. Wary.

Diane opened by talking about legacy, about how much the business had meant to John. Michael talked about sustainability, about needing clear authority to make decisions that were now beyond the day-to-day.

And then Emily spoke.

"I don't want the business," she said, voice even, strong. "I never did. But I don't want to feel like I was erased either. I just want to know that Dad would have been proud of both of us."

The words cracked the tension wide open.

For the first time in months, the family looked at each other, not as owners or heirs—but as people mourning the same man.

In that space, we found a path.

We mapped out a phased equity transfer. Diane would retain a substantial ownership stake initially, offering her security and involvement. Michael would buy into increasing ownership over time, building control without breaking family trust. Emily would receive a financial settlement—smaller, but deeply symbolic.

The plan wasn't perfect. It wasn't painless. But it was right.

Today, Michael owns the business outright. He's doubled its size since John's passing, honoring the foundation while steering it into a new era. Diane remains an honored figure in the company's story, no longer in the driver's seat, but forever present in the rearview mirror.

Emily visits often, not to manage, but simply to belong.

With the financial clarity that planning brought, Diane also found something unexpected: freedom.

At the family meeting, after Emily shared her thoughts, something changed for Diane, who had been holding tight to ownership as a symbol of her life with John. She finally breathed. "I've been trying to honor your father," she said, "but I haven't asked myself what honoring this family really looks like now."

With that, the tone shifted. We mapped out an ownership plan that respected effort and preserved harmony. Michael would earn control. Emily would be acknowledged and cared for. Diane would remain part of the company—but without the weight of daily responsibility.

And with that freedom, something awakened in Diane.

Over the years, she had always dreamed of giving back. While the business was growing, she had quietly supported local causes—donating to food banks, sponsoring community events, mentoring young men and women through her alma mater. But she never had the time or clarity to do more.

Now she did.

With the financial security that came from the planning we had done—and from the value created by the business's growth—Diane began leaning into her calling. She launched a donor-advised fund in John's memory, seeded by proceeds from her gradual business exit. She partnered with a foundation to support medical evacuations in war torn areas. She began supporting her alma mater in feeding underserved students.

One afternoon, she told me, "For the first time in my life, I have both the means and the energy to do what I was always too busy to do. I thought letting go of the business would feel like loss. But it's given me something new—a second chapter I didn't know I wanted."

The company is no longer the "third child." It's a living legacy—of hard work, of difficult conversations, of choosing unity over resentment.

What started in crisis became an opportunity: not just to secure a financial future, but also to preserve a family.

Because at the end of the day, money is for enduring. Not for trophies. Not for keeping score. But for carrying forward the values, the love, and the memories that matter long after the numbers fade.

Looking back, what strikes me most about John and Diane's story isn't just the business they built or the wealth they preserved. It's the hard conversations they finally chose to have—and the freedom that came from clarity.

Financial planning didn't just protect a company. It allowed a family to stay whole—and gave Diane the opportunity to use her time and resources to give back in ways that now define her second act.

That legacy—one built from a foundation of hard work, tough decisions, and shared vision—is what makes this story more than a financial case study. It's a reminder that clarity creates options. And options create impact—not just for your family, but also for your community.

REFLECTIVE QUESTIONS

- What conversations about succession, fairness, or legacy am I avoiding with the people I care about most—and what would it cost me to keep avoiding them?
- If something unexpected happened tomorrow, would my loved ones be clear on my wishes—or left guessing?

———————

WHY DIDN'T I KNOW HE COULD DIE?

Lawrence Sprung, CFP®
Mitlin Financial, Inc.®

"L ARRY, KEITH IS dead. It was suicide."

It was my father-in-law, Jack, calling on a Sunday morning in September 2004. In stunned silence, I tried to make sense of what Jack was telling me about his son—my wife's brother. I don't remember what he or I said next.

The news was devastating. Keith was only 27 years old. He had been the best man at our wedding, and he was my best friend. He was a super-kind human who always had a smile on his face.

We were all supposed to get together later that day to celebrate my in-laws' 35th wedding anniversary. Keith was going to get the cake. Now, instead, we were planning his funeral.

Keith was a beloved son, brother, and friend. Professionally, he was a hydrologist. He took great joy in being an uncle to our eldest son, Zach, who was a toddler when Keith passed. He was known for dressing in his Superman costume at the Boardy Barn, a popular bar in The Hamptons. Keith was fun-loving and always the life of the party.

"NO ONE BELIEVES I'M SICK"

Many people have a hard time understanding that a person like Keith, who was so outgoing and funny, someone who loved life so much, was struggling. Like so many people who struggle with mental health, his smile masked his pain.

Bipolar disorder is a disease of the brain. For years, Keith sought professional help. He navigated a series of diagnoses and medications but never found relief. I'll never forget how a few weeks before Keith's death, he and I were planting shrubs in our yard. He said, "I feel like I'm running out of time."

More than 20 years later, I still do not know what he meant. Because I was unaware that being bipolar could be deadly, I did not probe further. Back then, people did not talk about mental health, and Keith's insurance company wouldn't pay for psychiatric appointments. Keith often told us, "My own insurance company doesn't believe I am sick."

Bipolar disorder is a mental health condition that causes someone to experience mood changes, rotating between mania and depression. After Keith's passing, I learned that the rate of suicide in people with bipolar disorder is approximately ten to 30 times higher than it is in the general population and that 20–60% of people with bipolar disorder attempt suicide at least once during their lifetimes.[*]

Keith's struggle was made all the more difficult by society's perception of mental illness and the secrecy that surrounded it at the time. By sharing that he was bipolar, we hope to strip away the stigma and help others struggling with mental health by offering this as a resource for people, one that our family never had.

---

[*] Adam Rowden, "Are People with Bipolar Disorder at a Higher Risk of Suicide?" *MedicalNewsToday* (May 20, 2024), www.medicalnewstoday.com/articles/bipolar-suicide.

RAISING AWARENESS IN KEITH'S MEMORY

The evening after we received that devastating news, Denise and I sat on our porch, staring at the night sky, trying to process the fact that Keith was gone. We could not fathom that we would no longer experience the joy he had brought to our lives.

I will never forget looking at Denise and saying, "I didn't know he could die. My mother had breast cancer for ten years, and I knew that meant she could die. Why didn't I know that Keith's bipolar disorder meant he could die?"

And then Denise made a promise to the night sky: "You will not go quietly."

At the time, we didn't know what that meant—how we would keep Keith's name alive—but we vowed to share the story of his life and his struggle.

An old Jewish proverb says, "Everybody dies twice: once when your body stops and again when your name is spoken for the last time." We wanted to create an enduring legacy that would honor Keith by supporting other families experiencing this type of painful and profound loss.

Our vow to honor Keith's memory took shape just a few days later, after Denise and I were invited to participate in a local Out of the Darkness Walk for the American Foundation for Suicide Prevention (AFSP). That October, we walked the grounds of a local botanical garden with hundreds of other Long Island families who had lost loved ones to suicide.

That interaction led us to found the Keith Milano Memorial Fund, which benefits AFSP. Setting up a memorial fund within AFSP instead of establishing our own 501(3)(c) organization allowed us to focus on fundraising and outreach without all the paperwork associated with starting and running a nonprofit.

TALKING ABOUT MENTAL HEALTH LEADS TO HEALING

My family chose to be open about Keith's death from day one. Our honesty often shocked people.

Denise shared the news of Keith's death with a neighbor, hoping she would let the community know when Keith's funeral was going to be. Later, we learned that the neighbor didn't tell anyone, and when Denise asked her why, the neighbor replied, "I wasn't sure what you were telling people."

The insinuation was that instead of telling people the truth, we would make up a lie about how Keith died.

And at Keith's funeral, a woman whispered to Denise, "My dad killed himself, but we tell everyone he died in a car accident."

Denise replied, "I'm not whispering; why are you?"

Two decades later, thankfully, people are more comfortable discussing mental health and suicide. This is fantastic progress because talking about these topics leads to healing.

Beloved entertainer Robin Williams, who took his own life in 2014, also masked his pain. The 63-year-old actor and comedian brought great joy to the lives of so many people, yet he was suffering immensely. Williams' suicide led to a number of changes in how the media reports suicide and how people talk about mental health.

As people shared Keith's story and learned about our commitment to mental health, we began to receive calls, at all hours of the day and night, from those who needed support for family members in crisis. Thankfully, we have been able to help many people find support in their time of need. Navigating the mental health system is not easy. Being seen as a resource helps transform our family's loss into an enduring legacy.

Another major milestone in this journey occurred on January 1, 2005, when the National Suicide Prevention Hotline was launched; the name was later changed to the Suicide & Crisis Lifeline. Anyone in the United States can call or text a trained crisis counselor by dialing 988 at any time—24/7.[*]

It is rewarding to see the progress being made in our collective efforts toward providing resources for those in crisis.

FUNDING SUPPORTS OUR EFFORTS IN AWARENESS AND RESEARCH

By the end of 2024, we had raised more than $1.8 million for AFSP in Keith's name. Yet this effort is about so much more than the money. It's about creating an enduring legacy that honors Keith and provides hope to others who are struggling. It takes money to support outreach, fund research, and provide resources.

As a financial advisor since 1996, I have helped many families find joy in planning for their vision of tomorrow. They earn, save, and invest money not for the sake of accumulating money, but rather for the joy that money can provide to them both during their lives and in posterity.

Denise and I want our legacy to include encouraging open conversations about mental health, removing the stigma around mental health diagnoses, and supporting research that leads to better treatment and potential cures for bipolar disorder and other mental health diagnoses.

We hope the Keith Milano Memorial Fund will continue to aid in these efforts long after we are gone.

---

[*] The 988 Suicide & Crisis Lifeline, 988lifeline.org.

HOW THIS JOURNEY HAS TRANSFORMED ME PERSONALLY

Of course, the loss of a loved one is devastating, but I have learned that loss can also be transformative. I am now committed, along with my wife, to being an advocate, a voice, and a resource for those who are struggling or have loved ones struggling with mental health.

This journey has also transformed the way I work with the families we serve. Keith's death reinforced my awareness that none of us is promised tomorrow. My mother's death from breast cancer the day after I turned 23 was my first introduction to this harsh reality. This is why I stress the importance of joy in my work with the families we serve. I want them to save for retirement, with a focus on how those funds can help them achieve their idea of a joyful tomorrow. I also encourage people to enjoy today to the greatest extent possible.

Again, it's never about the money itself, it's about using that enduring resource to achieve ideal tomorrows.

This journey of advocacy has also made me more present as a father. For two decades, I have encouraged our sons to prioritize their mental health and to be a resource for anyone they know who is struggling.

When one of our sons was just 17, he stayed up until 4:00 am with a friend of a friend one night because she was suicidal. She asked him, "Why are you doing this? You don't even know me."

Our son replied, "Because I don't want another family to go through what ours has gone through."

In loving memory of Keith Andrew Milano
May 31, 1977–September 5, 2004

REFLECTIVE QUESTIONS

- What did you do today that brought you JOY®?
- How can your financial life help you share JOY and build something that lasts beyond you?

SURVIVING TO THRIVING: THE SACRED WORK OF SHOWING UP

Rob Duncan, CFP®, CIMA®
Steward Advisors Group

L IFE, FOR ALL its wonder and beauty, is not a predictable story. We write in pencil, and reality edits in ink. Even the best laid plans, ones forged in wisdom, faith, and experience, can be unraveled in a moment. And when the unthinkable happens, when tragedy arrives uninvited and unannounced, what remains? Where do we go from there?

This is not a hypothetical question. It is the raw, lived experience of many.

It is the story of Pippa.

THE PLAN WAS GOOD

Pippa and George had done everything right. They weren't wealthy in the way headlines often define it, with luxury cars, watches, second homes at the beach or in mountain ski towns, but they were more than fine. They had stewarded their finances with care, living within their means, saving intentionally, investing wisely, and seeking counsel when needed.

For over two decades, they poured their lives into others as overseas missionaries. Their faith, marriage, and purpose were intertwined. They had learned to be content regardless of their geography or material circumstances. George and Pippa always had their needs met, and although not extravagant, they traveled the world and formed great friendships.

Although initially they struggled to learn the local language and culture of the places they traveled to, over time they built a community of friends, both local and other expats, while raising three boys. They did life together with friends, crying through the hard times, and celebrating simple joys with people who knew more about hospitality and faith than about comfort and convenience.

Their life was rich.

When their time overseas ended, they relocated back to the US. George, a school counselor by training and a mentor by calling, returned to complete his PhD. Pippa supported him and they both worked as educators. After working and studying in the Bay Area of California, George took a job at a university in Southern California. His career was culminating exactly as he'd planned: in a Christian university, teaching future counselors how to care for the next generation.

Pippa, steady and joyful, had reentered elementary teaching. They planned to work a few more years, reaching full Social Security and Medicare eligibility. The favorable real estate market and the timing of their move from the Bay Area meant their house was paid off. Their retirement plan wasn't a Florida condo or golf club membership. No, George and Pippa dreamed of spending a few months every year traveling, not for leisure, but for love. They would go to the places they had served, staying with friends, caring for kids, painting walls, bringing laughter, and lightening burdens. Their bucket list was filled with names, not places.

They had a plan. It was beautiful, selfless, and ready for the next chapter.

Until the morning George didn't wake up.

MAN PLANS, GOD LAUGHS

There are moments in life that language fails to capture. Pippa's world changed in a single breath she took without George beside her. Death has a way of not asking permission. It didn't consult the spreadsheets, the calendar, or the dream journal. It just arrived.

This is the sacred space of financial advising that few talk about. Real planning doesn't start with asset allocation; it begins with empathy. It begins with being present. It begins with listening: to words, to silence, to sobs, and to sacred memories. And it continues, slowly, faithfully, into the new season of life that no one planned for.

George and Pippa planned well. On the day George died, delivered in the mail was the finalized copy of their estate plan they had recently updated since returning to the States. Even in the midst of her grief, Pippa was reminded of how well George had planned and cared for her.

THE MINISTRY OF PRESENCE

When Pippa sat across from me it was over two years since George had passed. Even after such a period, the loss was fresh, and the tears still flowed. She wasn't ready for a new plan. What she needed wasn't a portfolio review. She needed a witness. Someone to sit with the weight of what was lost. Someone to remember that George wasn't just a name on a beneficiary form, but a partner, a co-laborer, a best friend.

What we often fail to understand in the financial world is that transitions aren't just logistical, they're deeply emotional and spiritual. Pippa had to redefine her identity, her future, and her role in a life that no longer followed the script, the plan that she and George had created. We didn't rush this process. We honored it.

A DIFFERENT KIND OF THRIVING

There is a kind of thriving that doesn't look like success to the world. It doesn't come with bigger houses or jet-setting vacations. It comes when life is rebuilt around what matters most. For Pippa, thriving didn't mean leaving grief behind. It meant carrying it with grace, with purpose, and with service.

I remember as we talked, the moment when the tears went away. As a former missionary myself, her stories of living overseas and the joy that it brought, resonated with me. Pippa shared a dream she thought had died with George. "We always wanted to travel and help people. It was never just for us. We wanted to serve."

"Tell me more about that." I asked.

As she spoke, her countenance literally brightened. Her voice became stronger. She spoke faster and with passion. She was alive with excitement.

I knew this was a key moment. Yet, it was still hard. She admitted, "I don't know how to do that without him."

We sat in silence for a bit. Then I asked, "What if it's not about doing it without him, but for him? With him in spirit? Wouldn't George be thrilled you were continuing to live your dream?"

"But can I even afford to do this?" Pippa asked. With that last question I knew we had turned a corner and we began to plan her new future.

FROM GRIEF TO GIVING

Over the following year, Pippa took slow, courageous steps. It started with a list of potential destinations and times of year for travel. I set about researching flights, local accommodations in each location, estimating costs for ground transportation and other living expenses. With that total in hand, I worked it into her financial plan and ran several simulations.

It was a go.

First, she planned a domestic trip to visit family. Pippa used her resources to bring her kids and their families on the trip. She babysat, spent time with aging parents, cooked meals, and enjoyed quality time with family.

She returned and planned another trip. This time overseas. Pippa was no longer merely surviving. She was thriving, not by avoiding her pain, but by letting it shape her calling.

We now have a line item in her financial plan for one month-long international trip a year. It has become a non-negotiable element of her financial picture. She wrote me an email shortly after receiving word that her finances were sufficient for her to travel. She wrote, "Thank you for helping me to keep moving forward."

WHAT THIS MEANS FOR US

Pippa's story isn't just touching, it's instructive. It reminds us that real financial advising is pastoral. It's soul work. And if we're doing it right, we become guides through all seasons of life.

Over time, Pippa and I did get to the portfolio reviews, estate planning updates, consolidation of retirement plans, insurance updates, and tax planning. Yet even those took time. Each decision, seemingly logical and efficient from a financial perspective, was heavy with emotional connections to George.

A key turning point was when we involved Pippa's son into the planning process. He is a bright and engaging young engineer who deeply cares for his mother. He provided an objective evaluation and when he gave his blessing on the course of action we were discussing, Pippa was relieved. He confirmed that she was making the right decisions and moving forward as suited her.

We can't script our clients' futures. But we can help them prepare for the road ahead, not just financially, but also emotionally and spiritually. And when that road takes an unexpected turn, we show up. We listen. We grieve with them. And when the time is right, we gently hold up the mirror and ask: "What does thriving look like in this new chapter?"

PRACTICAL TAKEAWAYS FOR CLIENTS AND ADVISORS

1. **Create space for grief**: Don't rush the process. People in mourning need time to breathe. Don't be afraid of silence. Don't fill the room with data when what's needed is empathy.
2. **Anchored presence**: Advisors should be a steady voice. Show up consistently. Send notes. Check in. It's not about doing something big; it's about being there.
3. **Discern when to reengage the plan**: Timing is everything. There will come a point when planning needs to resume. Do it gently. Frame it as an act of love and stewardship.
4. **Help reimagine the future**: Invite them to dream again without prescribing. Ask open questions. "What brings you joy now?" "What would honor their memory?" "What do you feel drawn to in this season?"
5. **Stay in the story**: Stay in touch. Celebrate milestones. Remember anniversaries. This is how trust and transformation happen.

A FINAL WORD: FROM PIPPA'S VOICE

I asked Pippa if she would share a reflection for this book. Here's what she wrote:

"When George died, I felt like the story ended. But what I've learned is that love doesn't stop with loss. It reshapes everything. Serving others helped me find my feet again. I still miss him every day. But now, I feel him in the laughter of missionary kids, in the smell of paint in an old church kitchen, and in the peace that comes from helping others. Thriving looks different now. But it's real. And it's beautiful."

THRIVING BY SERVING

That was George and Pippa's plan all along. Death changed the details, but not the direction. And through Pippa's story, we see a roadmap, not one that avoids pain, but one that walks through it, toward purpose.

As advisors, as fellow sojourners, may we all learn to walk that road with our clients. Not just when things go well, but when life falls apart. The greatest act of service we offer is simply being there, enduring alongside them, until they are ready to thrive again.

REFLECTIVE QUESTIONS

- What does "thriving" look like for you in this current season of life?
  - Has that vision changed over time? What brings you deep joy or meaning now?
- Am I content with how I live, work, and invest?
- If life were to suddenly change, what would you want to remain true about your legacy and how you're remembered?
  - What values would you want to carry forward, even in your absence?
- Have you created space in your financial plan for the unexpected—not just for emergencies, but also to allow for emotional and spiritual flexibility?
  - How might your plan support you (or your loved ones) if life takes an unexpected turn?

SUMMARY OF
MONEY IS FOR...
Enduring

ENDURANCE ISN'T FLASHY. It doesn't always look like success. It looks like showing up, again and again, through heartbreak, hardship, and the heavy moments we never planned for.

In these stories, we see the quiet power of preparation. We see families navigating grief, transition, and legacy, not with perfect clarity, but with courage and care. We see how money, when stewarded with love and foresight, can become more than a resource. It becomes a companion through crisis, a bridge across generations, and sometimes, a way back to meaning.

To endure is not to avoid loss; it is to persevere through it. It's to move forward with it—eyes open, heart intact, still choosing to build, to care, to give.

Striving for perfection in life is unhelpful.

Courage is a far greater goal.

For courage, held quietly in the face of the unknown, through the hardest seasons, is the purest form of endurance.

DESIGN YOUR FINANCIAL LIFE: MONEY IS FOR...
Enduring

Write a legacy letter to your family

☐ Action: Write a heartfelt letter that shares your "why"—why you built what you did, what you hope it will mean to your family, and how you want them to carry it forward

☐ Why: This emotional context is often more impactful than legal documents alone

☐ Tip: Include your values, lessons learned, hopes for the future, and what success means to you

Schedule a family legacy meeting within 30 days

☐ Action: Set a specific date and time to bring your family together for a meaningful conversation about your long-term financial goals, values, and legacy wishes

☐ Why: Avoid letting critical planning wait until a crisis forces decisions under stress

☐ Tip: Choose a relaxed setting and prepare an agenda to guide the discussion

Document roles, wishes, and ownership plans

- ☐ Action: Write down who will take over your business or key assets, how ownership will be divided, and what expectations you have for each family member (whether involved in the business or not)
- ☐ Why: Unspoken assumptions can lead to resentment and conflict—clarity prevents problems
- ☐ Tip: Be specific: include roles, responsibilities, timelines, and contingency plans

Meet with professional advisors

- ☐ Action: Schedule meetings with a financial advisor and estate planning attorney to create or update your:
  - ☐ Succession plan
  - ☐ Will and trusts
  - ☐ Power of attorney and healthcare directives
  - ☐ Tax planning strategies
- ☐ Why: A plan that isn't legally documented might not be followed when it matters most

Establish annual legacy review

- ☐ Action: Add this question to your annual calendar: "What do I want my money and efforts to accomplish this year and after I'm gone?"
- ☐ Why: Legacy isn't a one-time decision—it evolves as your life and circumstances change
- ☐ Tip: Include regular family check-ins, plan updates, and goal reassessment

BUILDING YOUR FINANCIAL DESIGN TEAM

Shanna Due, CFP®, CCFC, AFC®, ChFC®

FROM INSPIRATION TO ACTION

F LINDA'S TRANSFORMATION from corporate stress to joyful purpose at Wrigley Field resonated with you, or if Tom and Stacy's beach house dream sparked your own aspirations, you're probably wondering: "How do I find an advisor who thinks this way?"

Maybe Jim's van life adventures showed you that unconventional dreams can have conventional financial solutions. Perhaps Leslie and Kyle's approach to "practicing" parenthood financially gave you a new perspective on major life decisions. Or Stella's hurricane experience highlighted the importance of having advisors who plan for life's unexpected turns.

The stories throughout this book reveal a powerful truth: money isn't just about numbers; it's about designing a life of meaning, purpose, and fulfillment. The best financial outcomes happen when people have advisors who understand that money is a tool for living the life you want.

Yet most financial advisors still operate under an outdated model, focusing on asset allocation, retirement projections, and accumulating the biggest pile of money possible. While these elements matter, they miss the central question that should drive every financial decision: ***What do you want your money to do for you?***

The difference between traditional financial planning and designing a financial life isn't just philosophical, it's transformational. Traditional planning asks, "How much do you need to retire?" Financial life design asks, "What kind of life do you want to live?" Traditional planning focuses on avoiding risk. Financial life design helps you take meaningful risks in service of your authentic goals.

Your financial planner should serve as the chief coordinator of your financial life, uniquely positioned to understand your complete picture; not just your investments or insurance needs, but also your values, fears, dreams, and the complex web of relationships that influence every financial decision. The right planner becomes a trusted family advisor across generations, someone who knows your life's worth as well as just your net worth.

This guide will help you find and work with advisors who will help you design your financial life; professionals who start with your dreams and values, then build a financial strategy to support them. These aren't just any financial advisors. They're advisors who understand that money serves five fundamental purposes in our lives.

THE FIVE PURPOSES FRAMEWORK: YOUR COORDINATION BLUEPRINT

The advisors featured throughout this book understand that money serves five distinct purposes throughout our lives, each requiring different strategies, team members, and approaches. Your planner's role is to coordinate these purposes seamlessly, ensuring that your financial resources support your life's evolution.

Money for Living means finding advisors who help you balance financial security with present joy. When Linda felt "drowning in stress" despite her successful career and substantial savings, the right guidance helped her redefine success and gave her permission to live authentically.

Money for Changing requires advisors who support you through life's inevitable transitions. Stella's hurricane experience showed how proper preparation, like building cash reserves before aggressively paying down student loans, becomes your lifeline when storms hit.

Money for Dreaming involves transforming aspirations into achievable financial realities. Whether it's Kendrick's career transition, Tom and Stacy's beach house, or Rocky and Lu's wilderness dream, the best advisors don't dismiss your boldest dreams; they help you find creative ways to achieve them.

Money for Giving means working with advisors who understand generosity as an integral part of wealth strategy. Julia overcame her fear of giving by seeing projections that proved she had more than enough, while Jon accelerated his giving strategy to witness impact during his lifetime.

Money for Enduring requires advisors who help create lasting impact and legacy, ensuring your values and relationships survive alongside your wealth through complex transitions and succession planning.

WHAT TO LOOK FOR IN YOUR CHIEF FINANCIAL ARCHITECT

The right philosophy and approach

Traditional financial advisors typically start with questions about your risk tolerance, investment timeline, and retirement goals. Advisors who design financial lives start with different questions: What brings you alive? What would you regret not doing? If money weren't a constraint, how would you live differently?

Consider the difference in how these approaches would handle your dreams. A traditional advisor might tell you that buying a beach house would hurt your retirement projections. A financial life design planner would explore why living near the ocean matters to you, calculate what it would really cost, and help you find creative ways to make it happen.

Values-based planning should be central to your advisor's approach. Exceptional planners understand that the goal isn't to maximize wealth but to align money with meaning. They ask questions about your life goals before discussing investment allocation.

Look for a **holistic perspective** that recognizes financial planning impacts every area of life. Your planner should be curious about your story, not just your assets.

Seek a **team-building mindset**. Experienced planners understand they can't be experts in everything, so they actively cultivate relationships with specialists. They should be eager to coordinate with other professionals rather than trying to handle everything themselves.

Most importantly, seek someone committed to **long-term partnership** rather than transactional relationships. The stories throughout this book demonstrate how the most valuable advisor relationships develop over years and decades.

Essential qualifications and credentials

Start with the **fiduciary standard**—planners are legally required to act in your best interest providing a foundation of trust that "suitability-only" advisors cannot match.

The CERTIFIED FINANCIAL PLANNER® certification demonstrates comprehensive financial planning education and adherence to ethical standards. This credential ensures your planner has studied all aspects of financial planning and can coordinate these elements effectively.

Specialization	Key credentials to look for
Retirement planning	RICP (Retirement Income Certified Professional)
Business owners	CEPA (Certified Exit Planning Advisor)
Portfolio management	CFA Charterholder, AAMS® (Accredited Asset Management Specialist)
Tax strategy	CPA/PFS alongside CFP®
Estate planning	AEP (Accredited Estate Planner), CLU (Chartered Life Underwriter)
College planning	CCFC (Certified College Financial Consultant)
Divorce planning	CDFA (Certified Divorce Financial Analyst)
Behavioral finance	ABFP (Accredited Behavioral Financial Professional)
Debt/cash flow	AFC® (Accredited Financial Counselor®)
Life planning	RLP® (Registered Life Planner®)

This is just a sample of the many specialty designations available. You can verify these or any others through official databases (CFP® Board, FINRA BrokerCheck, SEC records). Remember that the most qualified advisor on paper isn't necessarily the right fit for you. Look for someone who combines technical competence with genuine care for your well-being.

Communication and relationship skills

Active listening is perhaps the most important skill. Your planner should be genuinely curious about your story and skilled at asking questions that help you clarify your own thinking.

Look for planners who take an **educational approach**, committed to empowering you with knowledge rather than keeping you dependent on their expertise. The best advisors help you understand not just what they recommend, but also why those recommendations make sense for your specific situation.

Accessibility during both routine and crisis situations is essential. You want an advisor who treats your relationship as a priority rather than just another account.

Red flags to avoid

- **Product-focused conversations** that lead with investment or insurance sales rather than questions about your goals
- **One-size-fits-all approaches** that don't account for your unique situation or goals
- **Poor team integration** and reluctance to work with other professionals or dismissiveness of specialists you're already working with
- **Lack of transparency** about fees or compensation

THE CORE TEAM MEMBERS YOU MAY NEED

Financial planner/advisor serves as your primary guide, understanding all aspects of your financial life and coordinating with other professionals. They help you clarify your vision, develop strategies to achieve it, and adjust course as life changes.

Tax professional focuses on proactive tax optimization, thinking strategically about minimizing your lifetime tax burden while supporting your life goals, not just preparing your annual return.

Insurance specialist helps you manage risks that could derail your financial plan. Look for professionals who conduct comprehensive needs analyses rather than pushing specific products.

Estate planning attorney handles the legal structures needed to protect your family and ensure your wishes are carried out, understanding that estate planning reflects your values and supports your family's well-being.

Specialized professionals (as needed): Elder care attorney, business succession planner, trust officer, charitable giving specialist, special needs planning, student loan and college planning specialists.

HOW TO FIND, INTERVIEW, AND HIRE YOUR FINANCIAL DESIGN TEAM

Finding your primary guide

Start with proven practitioners: The financial planners profiled throughout this book have demonstrated their commitment to life design through real client transformations. They understand the Five Purposes framework and offer nationwide coverage with virtual services available.

Quality additional resources include:
- **Wealthtender**: Leading personal finance publication and financial professional discovery platform
- **CFP Board's "Let's Make a Plan" directory** for certified planners with filtering options
- **NAPFA** for fee-only planners committed to fiduciary standards
- **Kinder Institute Directory** for advisors with values-based life planning training
- **Professional referrals** from attorneys, CPAs, or other trusted advisors
- **Community networks**: Local business groups, religious organizations, alumni associations
- **Content and thought leadership**: Look for advisors who write, speak, or podcast about financial life design

Preparing for initial meetings

Complete your homework:
- Reflect on the questions raised by the stories in this book
- Gather financial statements, current plans, insurance policies
- Clarify your goals using the Five Purposes framework
- Prepare your questions in writing
- Include your spouse/partner to ensure both perspectives are heard

Research your candidates:
- Verify credentials through official databases
- Review fee structures for transparency
- Examine their typical client base for alignment
- Study their philosophy through website content and articles

The interview process

Initial contact questions (phone/email screening):
1. "I read about your approach in *Even More Than Money*, can you tell me more about how you implement the Five Purposes framework?"
2. "What's your planning philosophy, and how do you define successful financial planning?"
3. "Can you describe your typical client and planning process?"
4. "What's your fee structure, and how are you compensated?"
5. "Do you have experience with [specific situation relevant to you]?"

Discovery meeting deep-dive questions:
1. "Walk me through your discovery process. How do you learn what matters most to me?"

Green flag responses: "I spend significant time understanding your story, values, and life experiences before we discuss any financial products."

Red flag responses: "Let me start by analyzing your current portfolio allocation."

2. "Can you share an example of how you've helped someone pursue a dream that seemed financially challenging?"

Listen for creativity, empathy, and focus on making dreams possible rather than explaining why they're impractical. The advisor should demonstrate innovative solutions, not just conventional wisdom.

Follow-up: "What was the biggest obstacle in that situation, and how did you help overcome it?"

3. "What's your philosophy on balancing financial security with enjoying life today?"

Look for answers that acknowledge both the importance of security and the danger of deferring all joy until "someday." The best advisors understand that security and fulfillment are complementary when approached thoughtfully.

Follow-up: "Can you give me an example of when you've helped someone spend money on something that made them happier?"

4. "How do you handle major life transitions with clients?"

The right advisor should have experience with job losses, health crises, divorce, death of a spouse, career changes, and other major transitions; understanding these moments require both financial expertise and emotional support.

Follow-up: "Tell me about a time when a client's plan had to change dramatically. How did you help them navigate that?"

5. "How do you work with other professionals in my financial life?"

Look for specific examples of coordination with estate attorneys, tax professionals, insurance specialists, and other advisors. The best advisors see themselves as team leaders, not solo practitioners.

Follow-up: "What happens if I already have relationships with other professionals, you don't typically work with?"

What to observe during meetings

Pay attention to what **wasn't** said and how they conducted themselves:

Positive indicators:
- They listened more than they talked
- They asked about your story, not just your numbers
- They inquired about your values and life goals
- They expressed genuine curiosity about your situation
- They explained things clearly without jargon
- You felt comfortable sharing personal information

Warning signs:
- They dominated the conversation
- They jumped quickly to solutions without understanding your situation
- They dismissed your concerns or dreams as impractical
- They seemed more interested in your assets than your aspirations
- You felt pressured or rushed

Understanding costs and compensation

Be direct about fees and compensation structure. Key questions:
- "Do you charge fees, commissions, or both?"
- "What services are included in your fees?"
- "How often will we meet, and what's my access for questions?"
- "How might your compensation influence your recommendations?"
- "What happens if my financial situation changes significantly?"

While cost matters, don't make it your only consideration. A slightly more expensive advisor who truly understands your goals and helps you achieve them provides far more value than a cheaper one who keeps you stuck in old patterns.

Making the final decision

Trust your instincts about personal and professional fit. You're choosing a guide for life's biggest financial decisions. Evaluate based on:

The Four Cs:
- **Competence**: Technical skills and relevant experience
- **Chemistry**: Personal connection and communication style
- **Coordination**: Ability to work effectively with other professionals
- **Commitment**: Long-term partnership orientation

Additional factors:
- Do you feel comfortable sharing personal information?
- Do they explain things in ways you understand?
- Do they share your philosophy about money's purpose?
- Do you understand how they work?

YOUR 90-DAY
ACTION PLAN

Immediate Steps (Week 1–2):
- ☐ Complete Reflection Questions in the book
- ☐ Gather all financial documents
- ☐ Create your list of potential advisors
- ☐ Prepare your interview questions

Research Phase (Week 3–4):
- ☐ Verify credentials for your top candidates
- ☐ Review their online content and philosophy
- ☐ Make initial contact calls
- ☐ Schedule discovery meetings with your top two to three choices

Interview Phase (Week 5–6):
- ☐ Conduct discovery meetings
- ☐ Ask for references and check them
- ☐ Compare approaches and fee structures
- ☐ Make your decision

Onboarding (Week 7–12):
- ☐ Complete comprehensive planning process
- ☐ Meet other team members as needed
- ☐ Establish ongoing communication rhythm
- ☐ Schedule first quarterly review

CONCLUSION: YOUR MONEY, YOUR DREAMS, YOUR TEAM

W HEN YOU WORK with the right financial planner and team, your money stops being a source of anxiety and becomes a tool for creating the life you actually want. Beyond the spreadsheets and optimization strategies lies something more valuable: the peace of mind that comes from knowing your financial resources serve your deepest values and highest aspirations.

The advisors featured throughout this book have already demonstrated their ability to help clients like Pippa find refreshed purpose, like Brian and Avery achieve their dreams, and like Stella navigate life's storms. They understand that money serves five distinct purposes and have proven their ability to coordinate comprehensive planning that honors all of them.

Look for professionals who understand that money is a tool for creating meaning, not an end in itself. Seek advisors who are curious about your story, committed to your success, and creative in finding solutions to complex challenges. Choose team members who work collaboratively, communicate clearly, and inspire confidence in your ability to achieve your goals.

Remember that you're not looking for perfection, you're looking for professionals who will walk with you through life's journey and help ensure your money serves your highest priorities and deepest dreams. The right team will make your aspirations feel not merely possible, but inevitable.

Your financial design team is waiting to be built. The frameworks, questions, and processes you need have been laid out in detail above. The only remaining question is: ***When will you take the first step toward designing a financial life that truly serves the life you want to live?***

ABOUT US

EDITOR

Shanna Due, CFP®, CCFC, AFC®, ChFC®

Founder and Lead College Planner
Due Financial
Virtual services available.

Shanna Due is a Certified College Financial Consultant (CCFC), CERTIFIED FINANCIAL PLANNER® professional, and Accredited Financial Counselor®. She is the founder of Due Financial, the editor of *More Than Money*, and an advisor for The Braun Financial Literacy Program at the Boehly Center, Mason School of Business, College of William & Mary.

Shanna guides parents and students through the complex financial aid landscape so families can make smart, informed decisions without sacrificing retirement plans or limiting a student's future with unnecessary debt. She brings clarity, confidence, and strategy to one of the biggest financial decisions a family will make.

Shanna lives in Williamsburg, Virginia with her husband, two children, and rescue pup. When she's not cheering from the sidelines or exploring a hidden mountain lake, she's likely curled up with her latest book obsession.

CURATORS

Justin Castelli, RLP®, CFP®

Financial Advisor and Guide
Santiago—Fishers, IN
In-person and virtual services available.

Justin Castelli, RLP®, CFP® is a financial advisor, guide, creator, and founder of Santiago, a firm rooted in the belief that money is a tool for living an authentic, purpose-driven life. Through his AlignedLife framework, Justin guides individuals to align their finances with their spirit, mind, and body—helping them remember who they are and why they're here. A devoted husband and father, he sees his work not just as planning, but also as a sacred invitation to live with intention, clarity, and deep fulfillment. To learn more about Justin and his work at Santiago visit www.santiago.life.

Taylor Schulte, CFP®

Founder and CEO
Define Financial

Taylor Schulte, CFP® is the founder of Define Financial, a fee-only financial planning firm dedicated to helping people over age 50 lower taxes, invest smarter, and retire with confidence. He's also the co-founder of the Advisors Growing as a Community (The AGC) and host of the *Stay Wealthy Retirement Show*, a *Forbes* top ten podcast. Schulte was named the #2 top independent financial advisor by Investopedia in 2022. His contributions are regularly featured in Kiplinger, *Business Insider*, and CNN.

CONTRIBUTORS

Tyler Aubrey, CFP®

Partner, Lead Advisor
Define Financial—San Diego, CA
In-person and virtual services available.

At Define Financial, a San Diego-based RIA, Tyler and team specialize in providing personalized tax planning for retirees over the age of 50 to ensure they don't overpay the IRS in retirement. The Define team works tirelessly to simplify complex tax planning, retirement-income strategies, and portfolio construction.

A career changer with a finance and engineering background in naval and commercial shipbuilding, Tyler brings lean manufacturing efficiency to financial planning, creating scalable systems and concise yet highly personalized client deliverables.

A San Diego native, Tyler enjoys life with his wife, two sons, and their border collie-terrier mix, Stella. Tyler is a huge football fan and loves catching all seven hours of NFL RedZone's commercial-free football on Fall Sundays. True to his hands-on nature, Tyler boldly takes on several DIY home projects, from installing turf in his yard, building a retaining wall, installing recessed lighting, building new cabinets in the garage, and so on.

Nick Covyeau, CFP®

Founder
Swell Financial—Costa Mesa, CA
In-person and virtual services available.

Nick Covyeau, CFP®, is a fee-only financial planner and the founder of Swell Financial, where he helps families approaching retirement lower taxes, simplify investments, and align their money with what matters most. Married to a licensed therapist and surrounded by several other therapists in the family, Nick brings a unique, personable approach to financial planning—starting by helping clients reflect inward and explore their values before diving into the specifics of the financial plan, so they can intentionally design a deeply meaningful next chapter of their life.

He writes regularly about retirement tax strategies, generosity, and purposeful living. Nick co-hosts the *Real Personal Finance* podcast and runs a retirement-focused YouTube channel (@swellFP). He lives in Costa Mesa, California, with his wife, Kristin, and their son, Briggs, where they can often be found chasing the next perfect wave, hiking local trails, or tracking down their latest favorite restaurant on Yelp.

Jessica Davis, CFP®

Financial Advisor
Peterson Row Advisory—Dayton, OH
In-person and virtual services available.

Jessica Davis, CFP®, is a financial planner and investment adviser based in Dayton, Ohio, serving clients across the country. As a co-founder of Peterson Row Advisory, she partners with her longtime mentor, Christine Tenbarge, CFP®, to help individuals and families make smart, confident financial decisions—especially around retirement, investing, and building wealth.

Jessica believes financial planning should be approachable and empowering—not intimidating. Her mission is to help clients gain clarity and confidence in the choices that shape their financial future. She's known for her thoughtful, down-to-earth style and her deep commitment to financial literacy and fiduciary care. You can connect with Jessica at petersonrow.com.

Outside of work, Jessica enjoys playing volleyball and spending time with her husband, Brandon, and their yellow lab, Mango.

Jessica offers investment advisory services through Westminster Financial Advisory and is a registered representative with Westminster Financial Securities, Inc., Member FINRA/SIPC. Peterson Row Advisory is a separate and independent entity.

Robert Duncan, CFP®, CIMA®

President
Steward Advisors Group—Clifton Park, NY
In-person and virtual services available.

Rob Duncan is a CERTIFIED FINANCIAL PLANNER® professional, a Certified Investment Management Analyst (CIMA®), and a Tax Planning Certified Professional (TPCP®) with a heart for serving investors and families. He also holds a Master of Divinity (MDiv) and is currently pursuing a PhD in applied theology because he's still trying to figure out what he wants to be when he grows up!

Rob brings together a deep foundation in finance and a genuine commitment to his faith, helping clients pursue their financial goals with clarity, confidence, and alignment with their values.

With more than 25 years in the financial services industry, Rob's perspective has been shaped by experience in the markets and from living and serving overseas as a cross-cultural worker. He offers comprehensive, financial planning and investment management, including retirement and estate planning, charitable giving, and tax-efficient investment strategies.

Deeply involved in his local church and global Christian community, Rob also volunteers as a coach to faith-driven Business as Mission (BAM) entrepreneurs. He believes investing can be about more than returns; it can be a tool for meaningful impact, generosity, and gospel-centered influence around the world.

Outside of work, Rob loves spending time with his family and friends, and takes every opportunity he can to travel and explore new places.

Scott R. Frank, CFA, CFP®

Founder
Stone Steps Financial—Encinitas, CA
In-person and virtual services available.

Scott founded Stone Steps Financial in 2015, a financial planning and investment management firm located in Encinitas, CA.

Scott holds the designations of Chartered Financial Analyst (CFA), CERTIFIED FINANCIAL PLANNER® professional, and Registered Life Planner®. Scott earned a Bachelor of Science in Business Administration with an emphasis in Finance at the University of Colorado at Boulder.

Scott believes strongly in giving back to the community as well as in his profession. Scott co-hosts a biweekly podcast, *Real Personal Finance*, in which one personal finance question is answered per episode by a real financial planner using clear explanations, jargon free.

Scott was named to Investment News 40 under 40 in 2019. He has also contributed to numerous articles on personal finance for the *Los Angeles Times*, CNBC, *The Washington Post*, and *USA Today*.

Scott lives in Cardiff with his wife, two boys, and dog.

Cleve Gantt, CFP®, M.S.

Founder
Gantt Financial Advisors—Daphne, AL
In-person and virtual services available.

Cleve Gantt is the founder of Gantt Financial Advisors, an independent wealth management and financial planning firm. A CERTIFIED FINANCIAL PLANNER® practitioner, Cleve is passionate about helping clients find peace, clarity, and confidence in their financial lives.

Shaped by his faith and by experiences in small business, healthcare, and retirement planning, Cleve helps his clients find perspective and purpose for their wealth. He is honored to work to help individuals and small business owners steward their resources well by helping protect, grow, and manage their wealth, while also being tax efficient.

Cleve holds a business degree from Auburn University and a Master of Science in Community Counseling from the University of South Alabama. He serves his community by teaching financial stewardship classes through his church, contributing time to local civic organizations, and as a board member for his community's Public School Funding Commission. Cleve also serves on the board for the local Financial Planning Association and the Estate Planning Council of Mobile. Cleve has been quoted in national publications about financial planning issues of the day.

Cleve lives in Spanish Fort, Alabama with his wife Fonda, and enjoys time with their nearby grandchildren.

Yohance Harrison, BFA™, CRPC®

Founder and CEO
Money Script Wealth Management—Cedar Hill, TX
In-person and virtual services available.

Yohance Harrison, Founder and CEO of Money Script Wealth Management, is dedicated to enhancing financial literacy and building wealth. With 25 years of experience, he empowers individuals and fellow advisors to take action. A Morehouse College graduate with a Business Administration degree, he specializes in advising healthcare professionals. Yohance is a recognized speaker, having contributed to organizations like the American Academy of Emergency Medicine and been featured on over 150 podcasts. Honored as an Investopedia Top 100 Financial Advisor and recipient of the Dr. Wes Curry Award, he continues to inspire and impact the financial industry.

Rebecca Jackson, CFP®, CPA/PFS, RLP®

Founder and Lead Planner
SeedSafe Financial—Austin, TX
In-Person and virtual services available.

Rebecca Jackson, CPA, CFP®, PFS, is the founder of SeedSafe Financial and a lifelong believer that money should support your life—not the other way around. She's a tax nerd with a big heart, blending sharp financial strategy with soul-centered planning to help her clients feel safe, free, and wildly aligned. Rebecca works with tech professionals navigating big milestones like IPOs, equity decisions, and what it actually means to have enough. When she's not geeking out over spreadsheets, you can find her hiking trails, dancing in the kitchen with her kids, or dreaming up new ways to bring joy, purpose, and peace into the financial world.

Greg Kurinec, CFP®

Founder
Pennant Planning—Downers Grove, IL
In-person and virtual services available.

The common thread that runs through Greg Kurinec's life is joy in serving others.

As a young boy, it came in the form of helping a neighbor by shoveling snow, mowing a lawn, or just bringing in their garbage cans. More recently, it was launching a not-for-profit organization that supports families affected by cancer.

Even better, Greg gets to apply his passion through his work. Since launching his career in 2006, he has helped people at or near retirement, through investment advising, estate planning, risk management, and watching out for their overall financial well-being.

A lifelong resident of Orland Park, Greg is a graduate of Purdue University's College of Consumer and Family Sciences, having earned degrees in Financial Planning and Counseling, as well as Selling and Sales Management. Among the largest of its kind, the College of Consumer and Family Sciences instills in students the paramount importance of forming healthy relationships with families and consumers.

Through his firm, Pennant Planning, Greg has educated the public on common concerns—as well as unique circumstances—that have arisen from serving clients on the financial frontlines. Greg has also served as an expert source and been quoted on sites like Consumer Affairs, US News, and World Report as well as in publications like *Newsday* and *The Wall Street Journal.*

In 2012, after his mother, Jeanne, lost her life to cancer, Greg founded Jeanne's Journey for Hope to help other families battle the disease in its many forms. Since then, the foundation has raised nearly $100,000 to help families pay hospital and medical bills or as income replacement if the disease has resulted in a loss of employment.

Chris Magaña, MBA, JD

Partner
IMS Capital Management—Portland, OR
In-person and virtual services available.

Chris, a partner at IMS Capital, thrives at working with leading Pacific Northwest nonprofits and successful families. Chris often jokes that "there are white collar, blue collar, and no collar families. We were a no-collar family." Growing up in poverty made him curious about wealth, economics, taxes, and business. It provided a real-life MBA (He later paid for one and a JD from Willamette University).

Passionate about advocating for the voiceless, Chris believes in harnessing capital as a force for good. His dedication to the community stems from two pivotal life experiences. First, becoming a father at 16 instilled in him a relentless drive to provide financially and emotionally for his pride, joy, and purpose, Samantha. Second, witnessing his father, "El Jefe" receive overwhelming community support after a life-altering accident deepened his commitment to giving back.

Chris champions nonprofits and shapes future leaders through hands-on mentorship. He has taught at four universities and frequently speaks to youth and community groups about aligning wealth with values. Known as "The Money Nerd" or "The Mayor," Chris is a member of the Oregon State Bar. He's an unremarkable angel investor passionate about advising startups, founders, and venture funds.

Cody Murray, MBA, CFP®

Owner
Stillwater Financial—Stillwater, OK
In-person and virtual services available.

Cody is the Founder and CEO of Stillwater Financial, a commission-free, fiduciary-committed firm based in Stillwater, Oklahoma. A native Oklahoman, Cody draws on broad experience—spanning accounting, tax preparation, fraud examination, insurance, investment management, and financial planning—to guide university employees through every step of retirement. www.stillwaterfinancialservices.com.

Eric Nelson, CFP®, CEPA

Founder
Independence Wealth—Voorhees, NJ
In-person and virtual services available.

Eric Nelson is a CERTIFIED FINANCIAL PLANNER® professional and Certified Exit Planning Advisor with more than a decade of experience helping retirees and business owners make tax smart, forward-thinking financial decisions. As the founder of Independence Wealth, Eric works closely with clients to design personalized strategies for retirement income, tax planning, investment management, estate planning, and business succession. His approach is rooted in clarity, simplicity, and long-term alignment with each client's goals and values.

Eric's clients value his ability to break down complex financial issues into understandable, actionable steps—and to guide them with steady advice through major life transitions, whether it's retiring with confidence or preparing to sell a business.

When he's not working with clients, Eric enjoys traveling with his family, spending time on the water, and making memories with his wife and their two children.

Justin Peek, CFP®, CCFC, CLTC®, AAMS®

CEO/Founder/Lead Advisor
PEEK WEALTH—Carlsbad, CA
In-person and virtual services available.

Tired of advice that feels like a script? So was Justin. After two decades in financial planning, Justin Peek knew families deserved more than one-size-fits-all advice and generic check-ins.

That's why he created PEEK WEALTH—a firm built for fewer clients, better relationships, and real advice that's actually useful and leads to greater success.

Justin leads a team of eight that serves a smaller number of families with everything from college and retirement planning to elder care costs and tax and estate reduction strategies. In addition to the culmination of advice and experience from advising clients for 21 years, he holds the following designations to best advise them: CERTIFIED FINANCIAL PLANNER® professional, Certification for Long-Term Care (CLTC®), Accredited Asset Management Specialist (AAMS®), and Certified College Financial Consultant (CCFC).

The goal of PEEK WEALTH's capabilities for you? To make your financial life easier, clearer, and more aligned with what you care about most. And the busier and more successful you are, the more important it is to never lose sight of that. In a nutshell, PEEK WEALTH works with you to: define your ideal life; curate the best financial plan to provide the maximum number of choices you want for that ideal life; and invest your accounts to both outgrow and defend against anything that might upset that ideal life.

Justin's team works with a wide range of investors with particular skill and comfort at investor portfolio amounts of $50,000,000 to $1,000,000. However, there isn't an asset minimum to work with PEEK WEALTH as qualifications are based on values, compatibility, and a minimum revenue requirement. That's something Justin is happy to talk through with you!

Justin lives in Carlsbad, CA, with his wife and two daughters. Justin is a member of the Carlsbad Chamber of Commerce, Board Chair of the Carlsbad Charitable Foundation, Advisory Council member of Scripps Encinitas Hospital, and member of Rady Children's Hospital Professional Council, and a donor to the Helen-Woodward Animal Center.

Justin is a citizen of three countries and was born in Toronto, Canada, raised in London, England, and has called San Diego home for over 30 years. He's a football (soccer) fanatic and a diehard Spurs fan. Be kind in your judgment of him! His clients describe him as candid, kind, occasionally cheeky, researched, and tough-loving. If you're under his firm's care, he will be very protective of your ideal life for you and he and his team will move proverbial mountains with whatever you might need. It's a very different experience clients enjoy at PEEK WEALTH. You may review active client testimonials at www.peekwealth.com/reviews or call (760) 705-1200 to say hello and learn more.

Emily Rassam, CFP®, CRPS®, CDAA, NSSA

Partner
Archer Investment Management—Charlotte, NC
Virtual services available.

Emily is dedicated to helping clients navigate the complexities of their financial lives with clarity and purpose. Money isn't just about numbers; it's deeply personal and emotional.

While she ensures retirement accounts are fully funded and taxes are optimized, her focus extends beyond spreadsheets. She encourages clients to dream boldly and use their resources in ways that align with their deepest aspirations.

Beyond the numbers, she's here to empower clients to make responsible decisions that honor both their present desires and future goals. Together, they navigate financial decisions with thoughtfulness and intentionality. You can find out more about Emily and her team at www.archerim.com.

Michal Skowronski, CFP®

Founder and Principal
Skylark Wealth—San Francisco, CA
In-person and virtual services available.

Michal Skowronski is the founder and principal of Skylark Wealth, a Silicon Valley-based firm with a global outreach. He specializes in helping high-income professionals achieve a work-optional lifestyle and in designing sustainable income strategies for retirees. Drawing on his experience living and traveling around the world, Michal brings a unique global perspective to his clients. Find him at www.skylarkwealth.com. When not in the office, he can be found outdoors with his dog, road biking, camping, or on the perpetual quest for the perfect cup of coffee to greet the sunrise.

Lawrence Sprung, CFP®

Founder, Wealth Advisor
Mitlin Financial, Inc.®—Hauppauge, NY
In-person and virtual services available.

Lawrence "Larry" Sprung, CFP®, is a husband, father, entrepreneur, award-winning advisor, author, speaker, and mental health advocate.

He is reshaping personal finance by inspiring JOYful conversations around money.

Larry founded Mitlin Financial, Inc., in 2004 with a focus on prioritizing the families they serve. The Mitlin name illustrates their culture as the firm is named in memory of Larry's wife's grandfather, Mitchell, and his mother, Linda. At Mitlin the mission is to help you experience JOY in your journey while creating a clear path toward your vision of tomorrow.

He is the author of the bestselling book *Financial Planning Made Personal* and the host of the *Mitlin Money Mindset*, a podcast that reminds you to ask yourself "What did you do today that brought you joy?®"

Larry is a Founding Member of the Investopedia Advisor Council and appears often in the media.

Larry, alongside his wife Denise, has raised over $1.8 million for the American Foundation for Suicide Prevention through the Keith Milano Memorial Fund, highlighting their deep commitment to mental health awareness. Larry values his family, and his desire to do right by his wife and sons drives who he is, both in and out of the office. A passionate hockey fan, Larry still laces up, often for charity games.

Jared Tanimoto, CFP®

Founder
Sedai Wealth—Irvine, CA
In-person and virtual services available.

Jared Tanimoto, CFP®, is a husband, father, and fiduciary financial planner. He is the founder of Sedai Wealth, a financial planning firm serving professionals, retirees, and business owners. Jared is a CERTIFIED FINANCIAL PLANNER® professional, past president of the Financial Planning Association of Orange County, and a founding member of the Investopedia Advisory Council. He has been named to the Investopedia Top 100 Financial Advisors list and recognized by InvestmentNews as a 40 Under 40 honoree. He also co-hosts the *For The Wealth Of It* podcast, featuring conversations on money, business, and life. He resides in Irvine, California, with his wife and two children.

Phil Weiss, CPA, CFA, RLP®

Principal
Apprise Wealth Management—Phoenix, MD
In-person and virtual services available.

Phil Weiss founded Apprise Wealth Management. He started his financial services career in 1987, working as a tax professional for Deloitte & Touche. For the past 25-plus years, he has worked extensively in the areas of personal finance and investment management. Phil is a CFA charterholder, a CPA, and a Registered Life Planner®. He helps women facing new beginnings flourish through life's big changes. His mission to empower women with financial education and resources arises from the fact that he never wants to see another woman go through the financial hardships his mother did. If this sounds like you, please go to apprisewealth.com for more information.

Phil is a husband, father, and fiduciary financial planner. Phil and his wife, Diana, live in Maryland and are the proud parents of four children—six if you count their two dogs. Phil enjoys spending time with his family at home, hiking, biking, playing disc golf, and traveling.

ACKNOWLEDGMENTS

This book exists because of extraordinary collaboration and support. Our deepest gratitude to:

The Harriman House team, especially Craig Pearce, for believing in this project. The AGC team—Hailey, Diana, and Brian—for everything behind the scenes and the marketing assistance that made this possible.

Wendy Cook for her invaluable help with the initial structure and storylines. Francesca McLin for bringing the final structure together.

Tim Dyer for his financial support and commitment to this project. Emily Rassam for her meticulous editing and review work that strengthened every page.

Our story jurors—Eric Bakin, JD Due, Brett Fellows, Stephanie McCullough, Rhonda Olson, and Brian Thorp—who helped us select the most powerful narratives from an abundance of submissions.

Most importantly, to the clients and advisors who shared their stories with such vulnerability and trust. This book is your legacy.